CAREERS IN INTERIOR DESIGN

fb

CAREERS IN INTERIOR DESIGN

Nancy Asay
Missouri State University

Marciann Patton
Missouri State University

Fairchild Books | New York

Vice President & General Manager, Fairchild Education & Conference Division: *Elizabeth Tighe*
Executive Editor: *Olga T. Kontzias*
Assistant Acquisitions Editor: *Amanda Breccia*
Editorial Development Director: *Jennifer Crane*
Development Editor: *Rob Phelps*
Associate Art Director: *Erin Fitzsimmons*
Production Director: *Ginger Hillman*
Production Editor: *Jessica Rozler*
Copyeditor: *Rayhane Sanders*
Ancillaries Editor: *Noah Schwartzberg*
Cover Design: *Erin Fitzsimmons*
Front Cover Photo: *Red Cover/Simon McBride*
Back Cover Photos: © *View Pictures Ltd/Superstock (left);* © *auris/Fotolia.com (middle); Altrendo/Getty Images (right)*
Photo Researcher: *Avital Aronowitz*
Page Design: *Alisha Neumaier*
Page Composition: *SR Desktop Services, Ridge, NY,* and *Alisha Neumaier*
Director, Sales & Marketing: *Brian Normoyle*

Library of Congress Catalog Card Number: 2009920409
ISBN: 978-1-56367-716-8
GST R 133004424
Printed in the United States of America
TP13

To our families, who motivate and inspire us.

—*Nancy and Marciann*

CONTENTS

DAILY BREAD

EXTENDED CONTENTS

PREFACE

This book gives you a platform from which to examine, detail, and further explore the burgeoning and ever-changing profession of interior design. There are many reasons for the unprecedented growth in interior design and this book analyzes those reasons in order to accurately define and predict future careers in the profession.

Careers in Interior Design explores various traditional, nontraditional, and new job opportunities opening up in the field of interior design. It outlines the education, preparation, skills, and experience necessary to obtain or create any of the many job possibilities.

We strive to inspire and provide a compass for career development, which involves acquiring a sense of professionalism, developing and complementing unique personal talents and assets, and analyzing individual strengths and weaknesses.

The purpose of *Careers in Interior Design* is to help match the individual with his or her most appropriate and personally rewarding career path. We describe job opportunities, specialization, industry growth, and credibility.

Interviews with successful interior designers illustrate the day-to-day challenges and rewards inherent in the profession of interior design. At the end of each chapter, key terms, skills and aptitudes, related career options, necessary education, and discussion questions all provide extended information relevant to the discussion in that particular chapter.

This book goes into great detail about the various responsibilities that come with each career option. We do not merely list the various careers, but go into depth describing what each job entails, including the duties and concerns of the interior designer choosing that particular career path. What can an interior do, and what does the designer need to know in order to do it? These questions are always at the forefront of each career decision.

Careers in Interior Design can be used as a guidebook and source of information for a career in interior design. It can be used as a reference book in a library, human resource office, design business, or career advisement centers; a tool for recruitment; and a resource for related professional organizations. In the academic arena, it is a textbook for interior design students of all levels, whether in a community college, a four-year college or university, or an art, architecture, or design school. This book is appropriate for students and other career-track individuals working or doing internships; high school, family, consumer science, and interior design educators; individuals pursuing a career change; current interior design professionals; related-industry professionals; and anyone curious about the role of the interior designer and possibly pursuing a career in, or related to, interior design. This book takes special note of current changes and their implications for present and future careers in interior design; these include:

- Increased credibility in the profession of interior design due to state registration and licensure programs, affiliations with professional design organizations, interior design qualification exams, and qualified education provided by universities and schools of design.
- The development of new products and materials used in the building industry, and the subsequent creation of many new jobs.
- The changing demographics of our society (aging population) and the increased trend of people wanting to stay in their homes longer ("aging in place").
- The development of the concept of universal design—spaces and furnishings created to meet the needs of all people. With the creation of the Americans with Disabilities Act (ADA) in 1990, legislation now ensures that all our citizens have the right to accessible and barrier-free design.
- Lifestyles change and interior environments must be revised for more workable and flexible solutions. Space, inside and out, is being looked at more closely by both home and business owners for universal design solutions.
- The growing healthcare industry and the research that confirms that aesthetically pleasing medical environments can positively affect health and well-being.
- The concept of sustainable design, which has become mainstream, and the public and consumers' demand for energy-saving products, materials, and designs. We live in a country with many opportunities and available resources. Like many industries, interior design continues to acknowledge and support the research of sustainable and environmentally friendly products.
- Continued research and increased awareness of environmental psychology, resulting in the expansion of the field and its application in the field of design.
- The globalization that increasingly affects our way of life in many ways, including the products we purchase, manufacturing, profit margins, cultural influences, homogenization of style and design, job opportunities, and competition.
- The continuing advance of technologies that have altered the role of the interior designer. The required skills, purchasing, promoting, sourcing, information resources, computer-aided design, education, and job opportunities continue to be affected.
- Public awareness and the increased credibility of interior design as a profession, broadening the designer's role and responsibility in society.

In conclusion, there are many myths that need to be dispelled and misconceptions corrected (e.g., interior designers do not move mountains or walls). The paths for new designers need to be marked, the roles defined and opportunities revealed. The voices of experienced designers need to be heard.

Acknowledgments

Interior design is important, necessary, and valued work. We spend 90 percent of our lives in built environments. It is not just the buildings but the people who inhabit them, who give the structures purpose and meaning.

We would like to thank all of the families who cherish their homes, where lives are lived and relationships strengthened.

We would like to thank the people who labor and are productive in their workplaces.

We are humbled by those who find comfort and solace in places of worship.

If you have sought knowledge in a place of learning, from a one-room schoolhouse to the hallowed halls of a university, we extend to you our respect.

If your health and wellness have been restored in a clinic or hospital, you have given the building true value.

If you have found relaxation and enjoyment in a place for recreation, we wish you continued leisure.

These are but a few of the places where interior designers invest their talents and efforts. You have allowed us to create places for the human spirit to thrive and we are forever grateful. You have honored us with your trust as we educate and practice our profession. Buildings are places of shelter, providing safety, warmth, and security, and we thank those of you who have brought them to life by your presence.

An Additional Note

We add our thanks to those at Fairchild Publications who helped us develop this book, including: Executive Editor Olga Kontzias, Assistant Acquisitions Editor Amanda Breccia, Editorial Development Director Jennifer Crane, Development Editor Rob Phelps, Art Director Erin Fitzsimmons, Production Director Ginger Hillman, Production Editor Jessica Rozler, and Ancillaries Editor Noah Schwartzberg. We would also like to thank our acquisitions reviewers, LuAnn Nissen of the University of Nevada, Reno; Nancy G. Miller of the University of Arkansas; and Janet Fick of Ball State University. Finally, thanks to our development reviewers, Tamara Phillips of Algonquin College and Seng Sengsavanh of the Art Institute of Vancouver.—*Nancy Asay and Marciann Patton*

CAREERS IN INTERIOR DESIGN

CHAPTER ONE
INTRODUCTION TO INTERIOR DESIGN

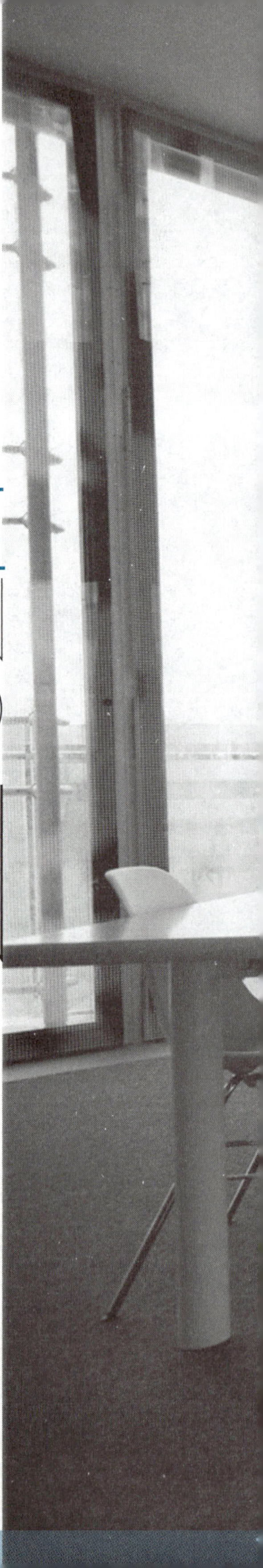

1

CHAPTER OBJECTIVES

After reading this chapter, you should be familiar with the many titles and the respective roles of the interior designer; these include: Interior Designer • Interior Architect • Interior Decorator • Design Facilitator You should also be familiar with the qualifications, responsibilities, and related job details of the interior designer; these include: Education and Accreditation • Experience Post-College Requirements • Professional Organizations • State Licensing and Registration • Types of Firms or Businesses • How Salaries or Wages Are Determined.

When students begin a college or university interior design program, they are often astounded by the vast amount of information they are to learn. The first days of class are for "myth busting." The study of interior design is not completed overnight, but evolves over an entire career. It is not effortless. It is not about the latest trends. It is not just about how things look. Wonderful design is not done by magic; it is created through the integration of very specific skills—though there may be a kind of "magic," or inspiration, involved in wonderful design.

Interior design is about how spaces function. It is about physical and psychological comfort—the creation of places for well-being. Interior design is about appropriate and well-chosen materials. It is about classic style and history. Interior design is about present and future needs. It is about people and socialization. Interior design is about beauty, inspiration, and creativity.

The designer is the one who makes all of this happen and more. You take a myriad pieces and parts, light and color, space and intended occupants, and you make it a home, workplace, place of devotion, school, store, hospital, or some other environment.

The role of the interior designer may be huge, but the steps to acquire the necessary skills are tried and true.

Education and Accreditation

Colleges and universities must meet state and national requirements in order to be accredited learning institutions. Obtaining a diploma or degree involves a great deal of time and study. It requires dedication, persistence, and, in many cases, a great deal of money. Through the accreditation process and by complying with established **standards**, institutions assure, at least in part, that the students will have the opportunity to academically prepare for real careers in the real world.

In addition to the school's accreditation, an optional requirement within the interior design profession for a college or university is **CIDA (Council for Interior Design Accreditation)** accreditation.

CIDA is an organization that monitors postsecondary interior design programs in the United States and Canada. This organization uses professional interior design standards that are recognized internationally. These standards are defined in their accreditation manual, which can be found on the CIDA Web site (www.accredit-id.org). The standards are very broad and comprehensive. Standard 2 states, for example, "Global context for design," and Standard 3, "Human behavior—the work of the interior designer is informed by knowledge of behavioral science and human factors." The CIDA standards highlight the breadth of an education in the field of interior design.

The CIDA Web site has a list of schools that are CIDA-accredited. This accreditation is prestigious. The most progressive interior design programs strive for this recognition. Even though CIDA is a nonprofit association, it is very expensive to have a program accredited and to continually update the accreditation. The expense and prestige of a CIDA program is due to the research, the lengthy review process, and the periodic assessment; all these ensure that an accredited program delivers the necessary educational value.

Each learning institution weighs the expenses related to CIDA against CIDA's relevance and importance to its interior design department. When potential interior design students are looking at colleges and universities, CIDA can be a definite draw. Increased enrollment means greater program growth, which amounts to more advantages for the student. All schools, CIDA-accredited or not, should aspire to those standards.

The educational experience in interior design varies a great deal from campus to campus. Interior design programs are usually located in the colleges of fine arts, liberal arts, or architecture. The number of hours required to complete a bachelor degree, associate degree, or earn a diploma can also vary a great deal between schools, colleges, and universities. The length of the program depends upon the type of degree, whether or not it is accredited, and the caliber of the learning institution, although there are some established minimums.

Community colleges, art institutes, and online programs can offer diploma or certificate programs in interior design. Universities, colleges, and junior colleges can offer an associate degree in interior design. An associate degree can usually be accomplished in two years.

Some interior design programs offer an extended study that will allow students to earn a master's degree in interior design. This extends a typical four-year course of study to five or six years. A PhD would require an additional minimum of two years post-master's.

Interior design programs are very comprehensive, leaving very little room for exploring other courses of study during the diploma- or degree-seeking time frame. The areas of study include: drawing and drafting, computer software for designers, history, art, residential and commercial design, sustainability, universal design, and so much more. If a student attends a junior college or changes his or her major to interior

FIGURE 1.1 Interior design students host Council for Interior Design Accreditation (CIDA) representatives and display years of hard work for review at a CIDA presentation.

design, the time needed to complete the interior design degree is extended in order to complete all the specific interior design degree requirements in a chronological order.

Within most curriculums, **internships** are a major educational component before graduation. An internship with an interior design firm or interior design professional can be an excellent experience and helpful for the student because it offers a hands-on learning environment. Internships also help students learn about areas of specialization in interior design.

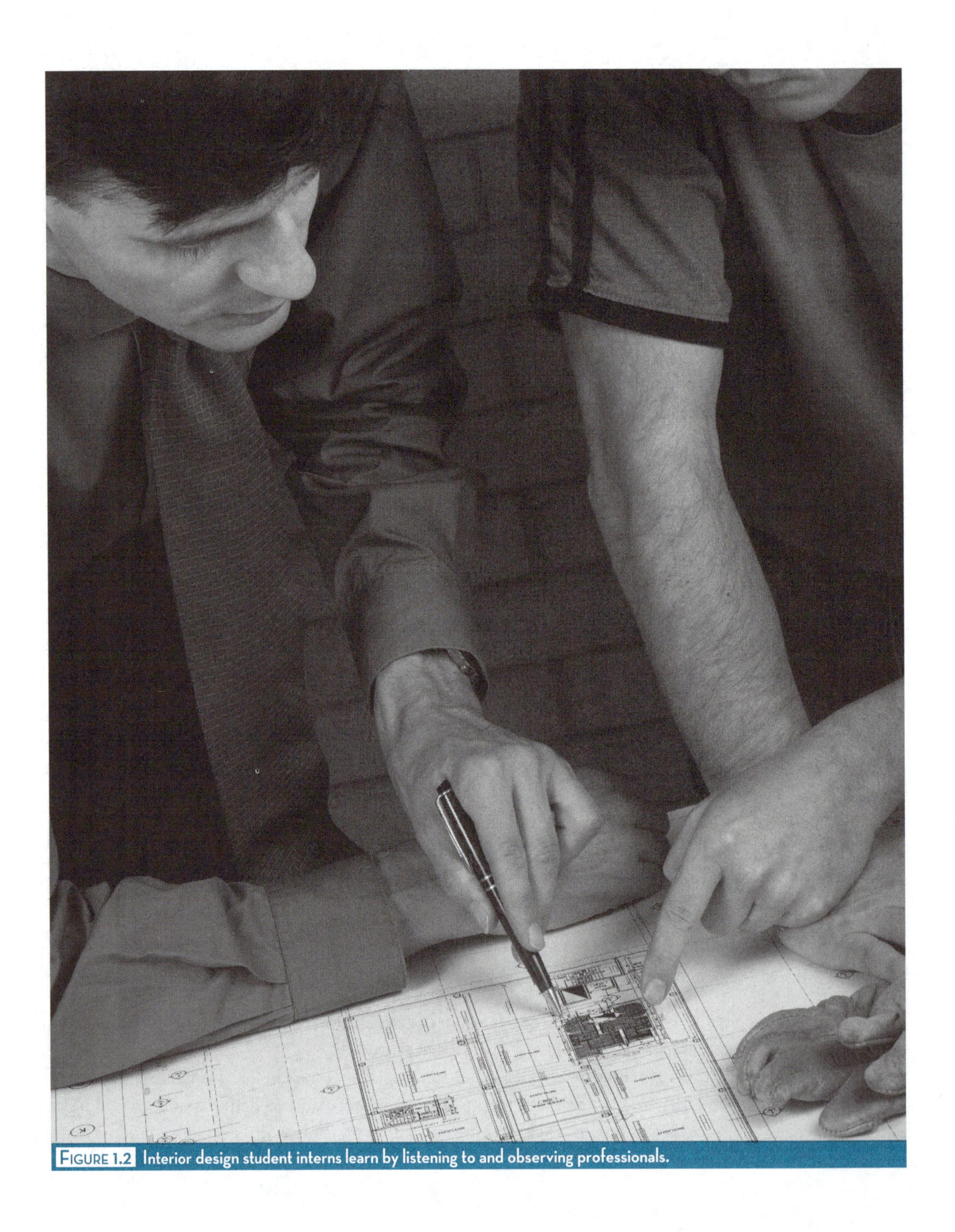

FIGURE 1.2 Interior design student interns learn by listening to and observing professionals.

Many times a student's internship experience translates into a job upon graduation. More than one type of internship is also encouraged in curriculums to give students an in-depth look at two or three areas of interest within the interior design profession.

CAREER TIP

Try painting, wallpapering, laying tile, sewing, or any other part of design services in your own home. You will have a better appreciation of what each person does. You do not have to do any of the actual work to be a successful designer, but the more you know about each job, the better you will be able to evaluate the workmanship.

Experience

Experience is the best teacher. It is for this reason that most colleges and universities require internship experiences as a required portion of the degree. After graduation, experience in any interior design career offers a look at that specific area and offers a network for changing direction within the interior design industry.

Experience is also a professional requirement before taking the **NCIDQ (National Council for Interior Design Qualification)** exam. The postgraduate experience must be done under the supervision of an NCIDQ certificate holder, a **registered interior designer,** or an **architect** who offers interior design services.

With a four-year college or university degree in interior design, two years of experience with an NCIDQ certificate holder, a registered interior designer, or an architect who offers interior design services are required before taking the exam. With a two-year associate degree in interior design, four years of experience with an NCIDQ certificate holder are required before taking the exam.

In order to assess the quality and level of experience an entry-level designer might encounter, the **Interior Design Experience Program (IDEP)**, administered through NCIDQ, provides a basis for evaluating a particular work situation.

IDEP provides methods of assessment, documentation, ways of quantifying a work experience, NCIDQ exam preparation, mentors, networking opportunities, and many other advantages for anyone working toward NCIDQ certification. Additional information on IDEP is available at the NCIDQ Web site (www.ncidq.org).

The NCIDQ gives precise information concerning the design experience necessary before taking the exam. The Web site also includes the precise areas that are tested. The NCIDQ exam is a two-day event and can be divided into three sections for completion. If a candidate does not pass all sections of the exam, the failed part can be retaken without retaking the successfully passed section(s).

Post-College Requirements

Many interior design careers do not currently require NCIDQ certification, state registration, or **state licensing;** however, most states require registration or licensing for commercial interior designers.

Interior design **coalitions** are in constant contact with the state legislative representatives and **lobbyists** who put together the regulations for these titles.

Moreover, the word "commercial" is increasingly being deleted from the registration name to include all interior designers in most states. There is currently little or no "policing" of nonregistered and **nonlicensed interior designers.** This will undoubtedly change as the relevance of the interior design profession increases.

FIGURE 1.3 Missouri Coalition for Interior Design board members meet their lobbyist and are introduced to representatives at the state capital.

Professional interior designers are qualified by education, experience, and examination to enhance the function, safety, and quality of interior spaces. Interior designers are part of the professional team that puts together any size of project—from the conceptual stage to completion. Other team members include: the architect; engineer; general contractor; electrical engineer; plumber; heating, ventilation, and air conditioning specialist; and many **subcontractors**.

CAREER TIP Have an open mind and be flexible when looking for a job. Interior design can be applied in hundreds of ways, from design interiors for custom planes, houseboats, or tour buses to select decor, to space planning for motor homes. Design a line of accessories or textiles. Capitalize on your talents and interests.

Professional Organizations

Professional interior design organizations provide a network for both learning and socializing. The major organizations are:

- Association of Registered Interior Designers of Ontario **(ARIDO)**
- American Society of Interior Designers **(ASID)**
- Interior Design Educators Council **(IDEC)**
- International Interior Design Association **(IIDA)**
- Interior Designers of Canada **(IDC)**

For a more complete list, see Interior Design Organizations, next page.

In addition to these professional organizations, there are numerous organizations that are for specialties within the interior design profession. Some examples of these are: healthcare, kitchen and bath, and construction management.

Local interior design associations are also prevalent in smaller communities where national organizations do not have chapters. This provides networking within the profession that is more convenient on a regular basis.

Each of the national or international organizations has professional requirements that are listed on their individual Web sites. Most require passing the NCIDQ exam, attaining **continuing education units (CEUs)**, and a financial commitment in the form of dues.

State Licensing and Registration

Licensing and registration are available in most states. Licensing does require that the interior designer pass the NCIDQ exam. The requirements vary from state to state concerning numbers of references and yearly CEUs. By acquiring continuing education units, the designer is able to keep up with new information, materials, techniques, research, and professional practices. A successful designer never stops learning.

States are working in the direction of limiting the title of "interior designer" to those who are registered or licensed. All others would be classified as interior decorators. With continued awareness of the education, experience, and examination requirements for interior designers, licensing and registration will become more recognized and respected.

INTERIOR DESIGN ORGANIZATIONS

- American Academy of Healthcare Interior Designers (AAHID)—An organization offering certification for proficiency in healthcare design (www.aahid.org).
- American Society of Interior Designers (ASID)—The leading national organization for interior designers in the United States (www.asid.org).
- Association of Registered Interior Designers of Ontario (ARIDO)—A self-regulatory professional organization for interior designers in Ontario, Canada (www.arido.ca).
- Council for Interior Design Accreditation (CIDA)—Accreditation to interior design college or university programs that have met established criteria (www.accredit-id.org).
- The Design Association (UK)—With members in 34 countries, this society holds a British Royal Charter for accrediting and representing professionals in many fields of design (www.design-association.org).
- International Federation of Interior Architects/Designers/Architects (IFI)—Provides a forum for international discussion among design professionals; currently in 45 countries on every continent (www.ifiworld.org).
- International Interior Design Association (IIDA)—An organization of interior designers from all over the world (www.iida.com).
- Interior Design Educators Council (IDEC)—An organization of interior design educators (www.idec.org).
- Interior Designers of Canada (IDC)—An official organization of Canadian interior designers (www.interiordesigncanada.org).
- National Council for Interior Design Qualification (NCIDQ)—The organization that administers the NCIDQ exam, which grants an interior design certification earned after formal education and experience. Passing the NCIDQ exam is part of this process (www.ncidq.org).

Registered interior designer and *licensed interior designer* are titles that virtually mean the same thing. Each state labels the profession according to how the law is written and passed in its state legislature.

Interior Architecture

According to the National Center for Education Statistics, **interior architecture** is defined as: "A program that prepares individuals to apply architectural principles in the design of structural interiors for living, recreational, and business purposes and to function as professional interior architects. It includes instruction in architecture, structural systems design, heating and cooling systems, occupational and safety standards, interior design, specific end-use applications, and professional responsibilities and standards."

A bachelor degree in interior design covers this content. It is very important that the professional interior designer understand structural systems, heating and cooling systems, occupational and safety standards, interior design, specific end-use applications, and professional responsibilities and standards. All of these areas are on the NCIDQ exam.

Some educational institutions label their interior design degrees "interior architecture." A practicing professional cannot use the title of "interior architect" unless he or she has completed the requirements for becoming a licensed architect. This terminology is confusing to both students and the general public. There is a distinction between an interior designer and an architect, each having specific qualifications, training, and skills.

FIGURE 1.4 This very clean space with few load-bearing walls offers interior flexibility.

Many interior designers do space planning, but it is not legal for them to make changes in load-bearing walls. When making interior wall changes, an architect or engineer must be consulted. The "interior architect" title is very misleading. The professional titles are either *interior designer* or *architect*. When an interior designer or architect has a degree in both areas, it can be accurately noted.

When the registration legislation first came into effect, some state governments allowed many architects to be **grandfathered** in. This allowed them to advertise as both architects and registered interior designers even though they do not have a degree in interior design. This was a concession in some states by lobbyists in order to get the interior design registration laws passed.

Interior Decorators

Interior decorators have no educational requirements. Many decorators are people who are artistically talented; for example, they may have a naturally good eye for putting color and patterns together. Anyone who has the desire and talent to become an interior decorator qualifies to be an interior decorator.

Before formal training for interior design was available, *interior decorator* was the only available role for this professional area of expertise. Now, decorators are those who might select colors, wall coverings, flooring, furniture, and fabrics. Decorators are the people "putting the icing on the cake."

This is another confusing title that needs clarity. The formal education of the interior designer is the main difference between the interior designer and the decorator. Public perception of interior designers is constantly improving; however, many people still call their interior designers "decorators." Sometimes interior designers perform only the decorating part of a job although they are qualified to do much more.

Interior decorators can work on any type of space but only in keeping within the limitations of their qualifications. They cannot call themselves "interior designers." As the general public becomes more aware of the interior design profession, credentials are becoming more relevant. A designer can verify NCIDQ certification, for example, by the use of the NCIDQ certificate number on his or her business card, mailings, and advertisements. **LEED (Leadership in Energy and Environmental Design)** certification can be verified by the lists that the LEED organization publishes online at its Web site. Because of privacy issues, not all lists for all certifications are available to the general public.

Designers Are Facilitators

The role of the interior designer is comprehensive. To reiterate the opening paragraph of this chapter, interior design is about how spaces function. It is about physical and psychological comfort—places for well-being. Interior design is about appropriate and well-chosen materials. It is about classic style and history. Interior design is about present and future needs. It is about people and socialization. Interior design is about beauty, inspiration, and creativity.

The designer facilitates this whole process by analyzing the situation or problem, finding solutions, assembling other professionals, and getting the job done. The designer's role is huge, but the rewards are enormous. There is research to be done, decisions to be made, selections found, and the design to be implemented.

CAREER TIP Be an observer. Whenever you have the opportunity, watch a painter, a framer, an electrician, and as many other contributors to the project that you can. Know what the allied professionals do and how they go about it. Be able to evaluate the workmanship of others. Then compile a list of craftsmen and professionals that you know you can count on.

Types of Firms or Businesses

There are many ways you can pursue a design career. When starting out in the field, it is advisable to work for someone else. You need to observe other designers in action, build your confidence as you gain experience, and get on-the-job training.

You may work for an architectural firm or a design firm, and, depending on the type of buildings that firm designs, you may work in any number of capacities. You may do sketches, find resources, create **presentation boards,** or engage in computer-aided design. You may be in charge of the resource room, confer with clients, select materials, or assist the architect in drawing plans. You may work directly with clients to select materials, interior finishes, artwork, etc. Each job is different, but all lead to the success of the project. You may work with a team or be completely responsible for certain aspects of the job. Whatever your role, each project adds experience to your resume, work for your portfolio, and knowledge for your career.

There are many different-sized firms—from 2 to 200 employees or more. In a small firm, your range of responsibilities might be quite broad. In a larger firm, your job may be more specialized, with each employee taking responsibility for a fraction of the project.

Some firms take on large projects while others design small buildings or residences. Some firms are mainly commercial design or residential, although others do both.

As an entry-level designer in a firm, you will have the safety net of the other more experienced designers, and the employer to cover the overhead and be responsible for the business in general. Many business owners delegate much of the design work, so they can focus on running the business.

After spending time working for a firm, some designers begin their own **independent practice. Sole practitioner** and **sole proprietor** are terms for owning a business without any partners. Some designers, however, go into a partnership. Regardless of how ownership of your business is arranged, when you are independent, all the responsibility falls on your shoulders and you are often the last to get paid.

There are many very successful and profitable independent design businesses. You can build your business from the ground up or buy an established business. Starting your own business often takes time to get established and there is always a certain amount of risk associated with a new business. The rewards associated with having control over your business are great, but the workload can become overwhelming, making additional help necessary for growth.

FIGURE 1.5 Many interior design firms employ a large number of design professionals.

There are many reasons for wanting your own business or choosing to work for an employer; these include:

- Family commitments
- Funding or lack of funding
- Independence
- Risk-taking
- Controlling your own destiny
- Being your own boss
- Carving out a special niche
- Changing your work situation
- Filling a business need

Whether you work for yourself or are part of a large firm, the interior design career can be fulfilling and profitable, if you are willing to educate yourself, work hard, and never stop learning.

FIGURE 1.6 Many interior design firms employ no more than five designers.

ACADEMIA AND THE DESIGNER

A discussion of careers in interior design would not be complete without mentioning teaching. Teaching is a rewarding career, regardless of the level. Secondary and post-secondary teachers work on a school calendar, sometimes have flexibility in scheduling, and lesson preparation can be done at home. The real rewards come from the interactions with the students. They provide the inspiration and there is joy in facilitating their progress.

Preparation for teaching involves first a bachelor degree to teach in high school, then a master's degree to teach in a community college. A doctorate is typically required to teach in a four-year college or university. Many interior design teachers have had industry experience, which can be beneficial for the students. Experienced interior designers bring additional insight to the classroom.

The need for post-secondary teachers is increasing as we see a wave of retirees. It is predicted that there will be a 12-percent increase in the demand until 2016. Wages for teachers vary depending on the institution and whether you are an instructor or full professor.

The field of interior design is becoming more comprehensive and the education more rigorous due to environmental concerns, the explosion of new materials in the marketplace, and the use of technology. We need good teachers to educate the interior designers of the future.

How Salaries or Wages Are Determined

There are various ways designers get paid and of course it depends on whether or not you have your own business or work in a firm, your qualifications, what services are provided, wage scale in the particular locale, and the reputation of the business. The status of the economy also contributes to fluctuations in wages. But one point is clear: the wages of interior designers are increasing.

The simplest way some designers are paid is based on an hourly wage. The wage scale depends on: experience, skill, type of projects, and the designer's seniority. Profit on sales is another way some designers are paid. Products and materials that are sold to the client are billed with an added percentage to cover design fees. It may be called **cost-plus**, commission, or percentage of sales.

Some designers charge by the **square foot** or a **fixed fee** for the entire job. Regardless of how the wages are to be figured, be sure that everything is in writing and the client understands how and when the designer is to be compensated. The employer of a designer establishes the wage scale upon employment or upon contract for services. The money exchange should be clear and documented, responsibilities defined, and dates of payment scheduled.

The contracts that are negotiated between designer and client are extremely important. They spell out, in great detail, exactly which services the designer will provide and when and how the designer will be paid. After all, the fees charged by the designer are well-deserved and his or her services enhance our living and working environments.

As with any career, knowing and abiding by professional ethics cannot be overstated. Your reputation and the success of the business are in part dependent on ethical and professional practices.

DESIGNER-CLIENT CONTRACTS

Contracts between a designer and a client vary depending on the type of interior design business and the nature of the client. Clients range from the individual owner of a residential property to small and large commercial businesses. Contracts also vary based on the extent of the services.

A contract is a legal document and can be processed through an attorney. They can be as simple as a few paragraphs or more complicated, calling for numerous pages. Contracts can be original or filled-out templates ordered online through ASID and other organizations.

Some basic topics to cover in any contract include:

- Names and addresses of all parties involved
- Description and scope of the project
- Services to be rendered
- Schedule and time line for services
- Basis for compensation (fee per hour, percentage of total project, or set fee) and method and timetable for payments of services
- Signatures of all contract participants

Of course, many other topics could also be covered on a project-by-project basis.

Interior Designer Profile 1.1

Mariann Chase, Interior Decorator, St. Louis, Missouri, and Naples, Florida

Mariann Chase, pictured below, right, has a very successful interior design business, We Design, in St. Louis, Missouri. She also conducts business in Naples, Florida, and has clients in other states as well. Chase has been in business, doing both residential and commercial design, since 1980. Having a lifelong interest in fashion and interior design, she started her own interior design business. She has a bachelor degree in education, but could not resist building a career doing what she truly loves.

Based on a solid foundation of experience in interior design, Chase offers some of her thoughts and opinions:

- Formal education in interior design is essential, but there are many successful interior decorators who build their business from years of experience and an innate sense of style. That sense of style can be further cultivated with education and experience, by utilizing industry resources, and by constantly being exposed to great design.
- Stay current in the industry by working through a well-established resource center.
- Working in large metropolitan areas provides diverse design opportunities, and having a good location for your business is imperative.
- The importance of formal education cannot be denied—for self-esteem, added credibility, personal satisfaction, and confidence.
- A degree, both a bachelor and an associate, can give you a false sense of authority and ability if you don't apply your education, if you lack experience, or if you have a poor work ethic.
- Most clients do not know the difference between a decorator and an interior designer. Decorators usually charge less than interior designers.
- My favorite aspect of decorating is the personal relationships that are formed and strengthened. Psychology classes are beneficial in better understanding your clients and their wishes; gaining greater sensitivity to their needs; and mediating, interpreting, and helping your clients discover for themselves what it is that they are trying to accomplish.
- The proliferation of interior design shows on television has given the consumer more confidence, but also increased the number of people seeking interior decorating services.
- People seek interior decorating services because: they don't have time to spend on decorating, they lack confidence, they lack knowledge, they have access to too many choices, or they are uncertain about their own tastes.
- Trying to keep up with trends is futile.
- Fluctuations in the economy may force clients to watch their budgets more closely, but people still seek to improve their homes.

SUMMARY

There are many reasons to choose a career in interior design. One must possess the genuine interest and aptitude and then pursue the necessary education and experience, but then personal and monetary rewards can be earned. Designers can enjoy flexibility in their work schedule. Projects are varied and interesting, and most clients can be a joy to work with. Success in completing projects is fulfilling. What more can you ask from a career?

RELATED CAREER OPTIONS

- Advertising Professional
- Antiques Procurer
- Architectural Space Planner
- Author
- Buyer
- Children's Spaces Specialist
- Design Consultant
- Design Contractor
- Educator
- Furniture Designer
- Greenhouse and Solarium Designer
- Healthcare Designer
- Historic Preservationist
- Journalist
- Kitchen and Bath Designer
- Landscape Designer
- Outdoor Living Designer
- Park Designer
- Photographer
- Religious Designer
- Residential Designer
- Restaurant and Hospitality Designer
- Retail Designer
- Staging Specialist
- Stairway Designer
- Television Set Designer
- Transportation Designer
- Trend Forecaster

ecause of the wide range of career choices in and preferred skills varies. In general, good good listening skills, creativity, being a lifelong ınd dedication are essential qualities of the

	Independent Practice	Presentation Board
	Interior Architecture	Registered Interior Designer
	Internship	Sole Practitioner
ıers	LEED (Leadership in Energy and Environmental Design)	Sole Proprietor
	Lobbyist	Square Foot
n)	NCIDQ (National Council for Interior Design Qualification)	Standard
	Nonlicensed Interior Designer	State Licensing
		Subcontractor

ONS

3. Analyze your own set of skills and aptitudes and decide which areas of interior design seem like the best fit for you.

CHAPTER TWO RESIDENTIAL INTERIOR DESIGN

AILY BREAD

2

CHAPTER OBJECTIVES

Identify both the significance of our primary residence in our daily lives, with all its physical and psychological attributes, and how the designer meets these needs. • Understand how and why the second home, resort, or vacation home should be designed for a different set of needs and goals. • Describe how the design process flows from the initial client interview to the completed project. • Realize how proper and effective space planning can influence the **aesthetics** and functionality of a home, large and small. • Understand how and why our **private and public spaces** change in size, number, and shape, relevant to economy and lifestyle. • Understand how the designer works with color in residential environments and how color, as one of the basic elements of design, can produce the most pleasing setting in a very personal and individualized way. • Appreciate how furniture and objects contribute not only to the aesthetics and functionality of the home but also become expressions of self. • Continue to engage in the environmental revolution affecting our residential design and products, and the **sustainability** of our resources.

We know that shelter meets one of our most basic human needs. We need protection from the elements, safety and security, warmth, and a place to rest. Our homes provide us with this and so much more. They can be a refuge from the complexities of our community and larger society. Home can establish for us a sense of place in our sometimes isolating world. It can be where we carry out the minutia of living, giving us structure, balance, and grounding. Home is also where we are rejuvenated, inspired, loved, and nourished by a wealth of memories created there. It is easy to appreciate the impact and significance that the home environment plays on our entire existence.

The convergence of our physical space with the psychological ramifications of the quality of that space gives interior designers their extraordinary responsibility. We as designers are not just creating beautiful surroundings but designing places in which to live a real, rewarding, productive, healthy, and treasured life.

FIGURE 2.1 This environment functions for a variety of family activities.

The effects of our residential environments are far-reaching, pervading how we feel, think, and act. Our reactions to our living spaces affect us not only while we are in those settings but wherever we go, because we subconsciously carry our attitudes about home with us at all times.

Residential designers need to understand how spaces can be created and manipulated in order to have a positive, long-lasting effect on the residents. We know from the study of **environmental design** and **design psychology** that the concept of home is not just based on the physical attributes of a house. In fact, much of our impression of a house is indefinable, subconscious, and intangible. But how do we create that which we do not readily see? Which tools, clues, and cues do we use to create a beautiful and functional home—one that we can carry with us in our hearts and minds forever, giving us sustenance, comfort, and a lasting sense of value to our lives?

The Primary Residence

When we talk about a primary residence, we are not simply discussing a homeowner, with a single-family dwelling on an individual plot of land. A primary residence can be, and is frequently, rented, temporarily or permanently. Many people never own their own home, but that does not make it any less important to them. The physical and psychological needs are the same, maybe with even greater importance because with lack of ownership, there may be a feeling of less stability and permanence.

FIGURE 2.2 Townhouses can be a relatively maintenance-free living solution.

DIFFERENT CONFIGURATIONS

The primary residence could be a condominium, a loft, a flat, an apartment, or any other configuration that meets our shelter needs. It could be manufactured, panelized, or modular. It could be new, old, historical, or contemporary. The primary residence could be built of brick or stone, wood or grasses, steel or rice paper. Other cultures might call home a yurt, chalet, icehouse, or teepee. There are earth homes, offshore homes, homemade houses, and the list goes on. Regardless of the type or style, simple or extravagant, home can provide us with an immeasurable amount of the physical and psychological necessities for living. As inhabitants of this planet, we all share the importance of home.

FIGURE 2.3 This yurt offers yet another living environment.

Residential designers play a critical role in the success of these homes and the value of their work cannot be minimized. A designer can manipulate the perception of space in our smaller homes. They can select materials that are sustainable yet beautiful. A designer works within budgets and can make suggestions to lessen energy consumption. They can create a functional space that has warmth and personality. Designers, with their knowledge and perception, can help transform a building into a home.

PRIMARY INVESTMENT

For most of us, our homes are the biggest monetary investment that we make in our lifetime. We save, calculate, search, and dream about our perfect home. We typically invest a great deal more time, money, and energy on our houses than we do on anything else. Our housing decisions affect our family life but also our accumulated wealth. Building equity in our homes is how most of us increase our financial assets; therefore, homeowners need to maintain, improve, update, and increase the value of the home in order to make it a profitable investment.

Designers can be instrumental in making positive improvements to the real estate of their clients. Space planning, fresh paint, and minimizing accessories are but a few of the many steps a designer can take to do more than just maintain home values. Designers can renew, personalize, and enrich a home in quality and in value. Whether the client is staying or moving, buying or selling, professional design help can protect and increase that investment. In fact, real estate agents encourage and even hire designers to improve the marketability of homes. As a specialty, a designer can become the certified "staging" expert in the real estate industry.

FIGURE 2.4 The constant desire for a new or different home keeps residential interior designers busy.

CHANGING LIFESTYLES

It is not surprising that as our lifestyles have changed—dramatically in some ways—so have our housing needs and expectations. The sizes of our families have decreased, but our houses are larger and require more attention. We have many conveniences that supposedly provide us with increased leisure time, but in many cases, because of the sheer number of these appliances and technical advancements, our homes are more expensive and complex.

The lifestyle of the average person or family is very active. We work long days, have many hobbies, engage in sports, travel, and generally stay very busy. It is essential that our homes run efficiently and promote the rest and relaxation that we need. Successful residential design can provide us with the home environment that is regenerative, calm, convenient, and beautiful.

FIGURE 2.5 Connecting spaces that flow in a very open floor plan work well for today's busy lifestyles.

BIGGER HOUSES

Our larger homes have many specialized areas. Floor plans are more open and casual. The living room of the past, with the home's single television, has given way to entertainment rooms, theater rooms, or large-screen televisions covering an entire wall. Interior designers have to plan and make suitable accommodations for all this sound and viewing equipment.

The number of people working out of their homes has increased dramatically in the past few decades. The computer has provided us with the flexibility to work from anywhere and we now have computers in the public and private areas of our homes. Home offices have become another essential space for many, even in the smallest of residences, although the importance of the space needed to escape from the office has not diminished.

FIGURE 2.6 Technology offers more people the opportunity to work from home.

People are living longer than ever and this has given rise to our concern with living healthy in order to ensure the continued quality of life. We now attempt to incorporate exercise equipment and/or exercise rooms into our houses. It can be a challenge to carve out that extra space and also make those spaces attractive in a residential setting, but a knowledgeable and experienced designer can blend in this varied equipment in a satisfying manner.

In the home of today, we want bigger and better bathrooms, often having more bathrooms than bedrooms. Walk-in showers, double vanities and sinks, bidets, an enclosed toilet area, spa tubs, and an adjacent dressing room are some of the extra facilities we now insist on for our bathrooms. Our closets have expanded; some are room-sized with built-in cabinets, chairs, shoe racks, mirrors, storage areas, cedar cabinets, and even granite-topped islands with drawers underneath.

In our bedrooms, we want a sitting area with a television, a fireplace, a beautiful view when possible, and plenty of furniture including a king-sized bed. These items require an enormous room, which further increases the size of our homes.

Many people enjoy entertaining, cooking, and opening up their homes to friends and family. Kitchens with several ovens, more than one island, and extra freezers and refrigerator drawers, in addition to outdoor kitchens and living areas, some with a larger deck than ever, further expand our family and recreational areas.

While homeowners enjoy all these specialized areas, we do understand and promote the choice of smaller homes. Our smaller family size and concern for limited resources have increased our appreciation for smaller homes. You can capture all the charm and use creative solutions to make that more conservative space truly meaningful and efficient.

FIGURE 2.7 Outdoor living spaces have expanded the size of our homes.

SPECIAL OCCUPANTS

Interior designers are finding that their clients have an increased focus on **universal design**. By applying the concepts of universal design to our projects, we create homes that our aging population can live in longer and more comfortably. If we make design choices in advance for the changes that naturally occur as we age or because of limitations (i.e., disabilities) that affect millions of citizens, then our homes can truly be our own without the worry of moving or the worry and expense of needing to **retrofit** our homes.

As the **demographics** of our population change, with more and more people living longer, adaptations to our homes are becoming necessary. We need to accommodate aging and disabilities of various kinds. Many of these changes and accommodations can increase the space needed. Home elevators, wider halls and traffic patterns, larger showers, and wider doorways are some examples of changing space allocation. Many other considerations need to be made as well: increased lighting, smooth floor transitions, lever handles, adjustable showerheads, and other products as prescribed by the **Americans with Disabilities Act (ADA)** and the principles of universal design.

We are providing more and more space for our pets, establishing special living areas created just for them. The number of products (furniture, ramps, washing facilities, climbing apparatuses) has increased dramatically in the past few years, adding to the challenges of the residential designer.

FIGURE 2.8 The universally designed interior is perfect for aging in place.

Resort Homes

A resort home is a type of secondary home that is used primarily for vacations. It may be located in a resort area or place of great tourist appeal, or possibly in a remote and isolated location. Often the resort home can become the primary residence after retirement or downsizing. A second home, usually smaller in scale than one's primary home, might also be necessary to avoid long commutes during the workweek rather than for vacation and relaxation purposes.

The expectations and goals for this type of home are very different from what we need and want from our primary residence. This type of house provides a "getaway" when we want to escape from our harried lives: a place to relax, enjoy leisure time, and entertain friends and family in a new and different atmosphere. Knowing this, designers work to create a simplified, comfortable, and low-maintenance dwelling, an environment more conducive to rest and relaxation. The choice of materials, the colors, and the space planning all contribute to that "I'm on vacation" environment.

Programming: Analysis and Synthesis

How can the residential designer help the client with the enormous job of planning and designing a home? How can we solve our housing problems?

We begin with analysis and information gathering.

The problem might be that the client is building a new house or just redecorating the kitchen. In either case, the approach to finding the solution is very similar: Simply, but in great detail, ask who, what, where, and why. You need to determine:

- Who will be using the space? Work up a profile of the occupants and find out if there will be other users of the space.
- What will the space be used for? Determine the activities, functions, space requirements, and other specifics that are necessary for the intended space.
- Where is the space? Map the location of the house or room, geographically and in relation to other areas.
- What is the reason for building or remodeling the space? Is it necessary, desired, or both? What economic factors need to be considered?

This is only a simplification of the **programming** process. A great deal of consideration goes into the interview and this analytical process. Residential design is of a very personal nature, meeting the needs of very specific people with unique and individual tastes.

DESIGNER AS PSYCHOLOGIST

The role of the designer in this process can be similar to that of a psychologist. You have to be a good listener and be very sensitive and perceptive to what the client says in order to design for the individual rather than generically. The client may not have easily defined taste nor have ever really analyzed what it is in a home that he or she is seeking. The designer takes the client step by step through the analytical process and soon attitudes, emotions, and preferences start to take shape.

It is in this first stage of the design process that the fields of design psychology and environmental psychology can be extremely relevant. But before we can find out the answers, we have to ask the questions. The information gathering stage can be lengthy but as the process continues, the client and designer hopefully refine and extend the lines of communication. It is the communication of all these thoughts and feelings that ensures the success of the design project.

FIGURE 2.9 Bedroom suites have evolved into much larger, multifaceted spaces.

DESIGNER AS MEDIATOR

The designer gets to know the clients very well and often acts as the mediator between the client and the architect, the client and the contractor, and any other participant in the project. The client needs to trust the designer, and feel comfortable expressing thoughts and ideas. The designer, in turn, needs to handle this information with care and, in certain respects, with some element of privacy. The designer becomes acquainted with the client on a very personal level and the two often develop lasting friendships, both personally and professionally.

Design Concepts

After the designer has concluded the information gathering stage—although more information may surface as the design process continues—the **design concepts** begin to take shape. Ideas are tossed back and forth between the designer and the client, opinions given, and decisions are made. In order to ensure accuracy, visuals are then developed. The visuals might be pictures—quickly drawn and informal sketches, presentation boards, material lists, renderings, and ultimately the working drawings. Communication is vital, both visual and verbal.

The goal of the designer at this point is to make sure that everything the client wanted is in the plan, that the problems have been solved, and that the desired goals will be achieved. Soon, the contracts for all the subcontractors will be signed and work will begin.

Space Planning

Residential designers work with the aesthetics and visuals of a space while planning how that three-dimensional space will be used and how it will function. The space in a home is initially dictated by the structure itself, then broken down and divided into specific areas, usually for distinct purposes.

Because of the price of each square foot and the sometimes very limited space in our homes, the organization and allocation of space is critical. The designer may begin with an open space, void of all objects, and by analysis of the needs, attitudes about space, and personal preferences, begin to divide, separate, and enclose certain areas.

PUBLIC AND PRIVATE SPACES

The house is divided into public and private areas, influenced by culture and personal choice. Our personal sense of privacy may dictate not only the planning of space but the placement and number of doors and windows. In general, a home is a private space where we live our lives out of the public eye, maybe only separated by a 6-inch wall or even thinner door. Within that enclosed space called home, we further close off private spaces. We leave some space, depending on personal lifestyle, open for public use. That public may simply be friends and family. Whether we entertain frequently, work at home, or require lots of personal space, the interior designer must determine how the space will be divided. Defining the activities of all the members of the household is necessary to plan and organize the space for the benefit of all.

FIGURE 2.10 The vaulted ceiling makes this small space seem much larger.

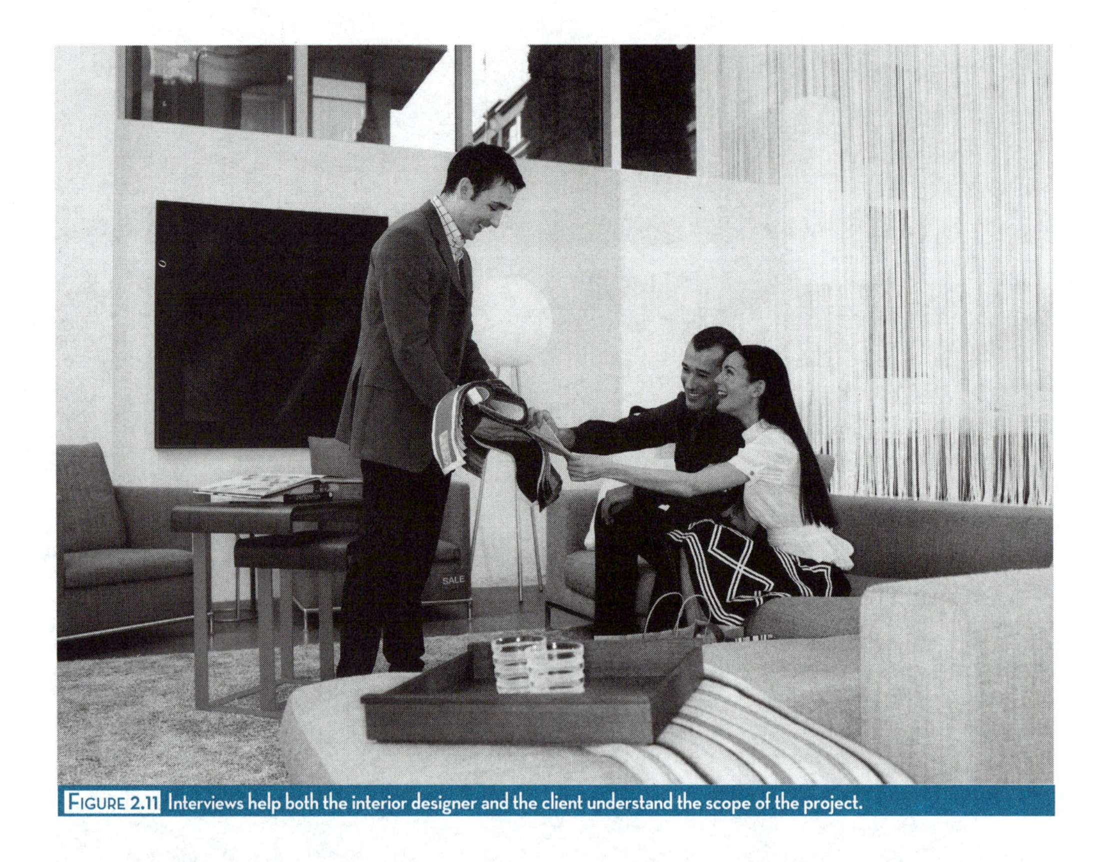

FIGURE 2.11 Interviews help both the interior designer and the client understand the scope of the project.

Space planning should change with evolving life patterns. Interior designers determine many design decisions based upon the number and ages of the occupants; these factors may also help the designer establish the style and type of the house. Some houses are more adaptable than others. Residential designers analyze all these variables and more to come up with the best solutions for each particular situation and its unique individuals.

Some other space planning considerations for the designer are the **International Residential Codes (IRC)**. These mandate certain space requirements for our buildings' kitchens, bathrooms, bedrooms, and other areas. The ADA also seeks conformity in accommodations for people with disabilities.

SPACE PLANNING AND OUR ENVIRONMENT

Because of our increased awareness of environmental issues and the necessary conservation of resources, spatial considerations are paramount. We are seeing a reevaluation of our need for more space in our homes and the public needs to change consumption patterns. "Bigger is not always better" and "quality rather than quantity" can be two of our guiding principles. We can successfully create environments that do not tax our resources or those of the environment. Instead of merely adding square footage, we can change our perception of space in a room. A small room can appear larger by implementing appropriate design principles and elements. Designers can manipulate and create the visual space we want. By organizing a smaller space, we can also increase the functionality of that space. When attempting to live modestly and economically, making better use of smaller spaces can be rewarding financially and psychologically. Smaller spaces require less money upfront, and are easier and less costly to maintain, heat, and cool. A smaller home can also increase family interaction and cohesiveness.

OPEN SPACE PLANNING

Open space planning allows for more flexibility than planning many closed-off areas. We have resorted to multitasking in order to get more production out of each and every minute. We need to create and enhance spaces that allow us to do that more efficiently in our homes. Our "great rooms" provide us with the open space to perform many different tasks in addition to areas for socialization, entertainment, and conversation. The "great room" or hearth room can be the hub of family activity and promote interaction between family members and guests. Designers refine these spaces and make them work for current needs as well as considering the future uses of that space.

Open space planning can be more energy-efficient, which is a concern of most clients. Lighting can be more effective, therefore less costly. Construction costs and construction wastes decrease with open planning. Designers have a responsibility to educate clients in regard to supporting our environment rather than contributing to its demise. Choices we make in space planning, material choices, and using our available natural resources in a beneficial way contribute to the quality of life for everyone.

Kitchens have historically been the family gathering place. The warmth, smells, and family interaction contribute to a sense of home. The kitchen designers of today need to plan for and support the fact that we still gravitate to the kitchen for our informal gatherings.

Designers need to honor our past associations and attitudes about home, while incorporating present needs, goods, and materials. The designer should also keep a watchful eye toward the future.

Interior Color

Probably one of the most exciting areas of design is color. Color is one of the most obvious attributes of decor. It can also be tricky and illusive, fun and perplexing. Like a chameleon, color is ever-changing, from one wall to the next, from one time of day to the next. It is difficult to predict, but can dramatically change the look and feel of a room more easily and less expensively than can any other method. Color selection is a main component of a designer's work and there are many jobs that have color as their focus: colorist, color forecaster, product developer, painter, textiler, carpet professional, and many others too numerous to mention. We cannot minimize the impact that color has on our lives and on the role of the designer.

FIGURE 2.12 This hearth room functions much like a traditional large kitchen.

COLOR PSYCHOLOGY

Part of the intrigue of color is how vastly different it can affect people. The associations, reactions, meanings, and perceptions of color can vary enormously. Color is very personal and can cause widely different responses. A great deal of research has been done on color because of the physiological and psychological reactions it can cause.

CAREER TIP Working with four colors or more in a room requires more expertise and creative thinking.

Some colors are more energizing—reds and yellows—while others are more relaxing, such as blues and greens. For example, the color palette used in a bedroom might be different from more exciting colors used in a kitchen.

Color can change your sense of temperature. While working in a bright yellow or red room, you might feel several degrees warmer. Conversely, working in a pale blue room may make you feel several degrees cooler.

Our reaction to color can be very personal and individual. Certain colors may agitate some of us, while other colors make us feel more passive. In prisons, pink has sometimes been used on the walls to make the inmates less aggressive. Color is capable of causing various emotional reactions based on association. Because of some experience, positive or negative, we may associate a certain feeling with a particular color. In general, we attach emotion with certain colors. Black can symbolize death, depression, and dark moods. We associate yellow with happiness, red with passion, purple with royalty, and white with purity. A designer would not select dark, somber colors for a person who experienced depression or mood swings. The emotional reactions and the meaning of certain colors can vary from person to person, but the symbolism we attach to colors is strong. Dorothy's red slippers in *The Wizard of Oz*, for instance, forever remind us that "there is no place like home."

FIGURE 2.13 The color contrasts in this space create a very pleasant visual. (See color plate 1.)

COLOR TRICKS THE EYE

Designers capitalize on the many attributes of color to use it effectively in their clients' homes. Color can change our perception of space so it is used as a tool to make a room appear larger or smaller. Cool, light colors make a room appear larger whereas dark and intense colors can make a room appear smaller.

FIGURE 2.14 The light colors in this room help give it a more spacious feeling. (See color plate 2.)

The magic of color can be seen when placing two side by side. The relationship between two colors can change how they appear. Color is relative and depends on the color placed next to it. It is affected by light, reflections, and shadows. Color depends on the texture it is on (e.g., smooth or rough) and whether it is on a large area or a smaller one.

COLOR CULTURE

The meaning and symbolism of certain colors vary by culture—cultures with which the designer may need to become familiar when working with clients from other parts of the world or clients who maintain strong allegiance to their heritage. We need to respect and preserve the cultural differences and incorporate them into our design solutions. In China, for example, red is a color associated with happiness and weddings and white is symbolic of death. In our culture, black connotes death whereas white represents weddings. Some men won't wear pink because they associate it with the feminine or lack of male strength. Currently, all over the world, green represents our need to conserve our natural resources and preserve our environment.

Color can have historical significance. Certain colors represent certain time periods in housing, different popular styles, and different types of homes, depending on their locations.

The designer's ability to work effectively with color, acknowledging both the psychological and physiological aspects, can greatly facilitate good design.

FIGURE 2.15 The historical color collection in this dining room emphasizes the period design. (See color plate 3.)

COLOR BUSINESS

Color, being the least expensive facet to change as well as the most impactful, is often the first thing considered when making design changes. In addition, fashion, whether clothing or decor, changes at a very rapid rate, and color is at the forefront of this continually changing market. Color forecasters work years in advance to predict the colors for upcoming years. Several huge firms do market surveys, watch every aspect of fashion and design, search for clues, and analyze trends, in order to accurately predict which colors we will be using in our homes in the near future. This kind of research helps drives the paint, fabric, carpet, wholesale, and retail segments of our economy and provides another area of specialization for the interior designer.

Layers of Lighting

The way that designers approach lighting has changed dramatically since the days of the lone incandescent bulb, ceiling-centered, in every room. Interior designers now work with many new and efficient types of lighting; there is a light for every need—every task, mood, wayfinding and/or signage system, accent, and other architectural requirement—and just as many ways to use natural light. Incorporating many layers of lighting in the home improves visibility and also enhances the beauty of the space.

Furniture and Accessories

When selecting furniture, the designer first assesses the needs and requirements for each particular area. We don't just fill up spaces with items that simply look good; instead, we have to determine the activities and functions of each room in order to make intelligent decisions about furniture selection. We must also be concerned about the movement in, around, and out of the rooms. Congestion, disorganization, poorly arranged seating areas, and cramped walkways all rob a room of comfort and make it very unpleasant to occupy. Regardless of how attractive a space is, if it does not function efficiently, the design fails. When selecting furniture and accessories, the designer must pay particular attention to the well-established **design principles** and **design elements** crucial to ultimate success. The principles and elements that designers utilize and manipulate are the foundation and building blocks of any good design, regardless of the type or scope of the job. The principles—scale, proportion, emphasis, balance, rhythm, and harmony—create the foundation. The elements—space, shape or form, mass, line, color, texture, light, and pattern—are the building blocks that further construct the designed environment.

The designer must evaluate the quality of the furniture, inside and out—its frame, construction, fabric, wood, and hardware—in addition to its style and overall appearance.

The client can truly express his or her own personal taste and preferences in the selection of furniture and accessories. We fill our houses with memorabilia, furniture handed down from generation to generation, collectibles, and many other items that carry a strong sentimental attachment. The

CAREER TIP Continuity needs to include both inside and outside spaces. Make all finishes look "on purpose."

FIGURE 2.16 Quality furnishings are considered investment pieces.

designer has to skillfully blend these items into the overall plan, filling in with new items when necessary and according to the budget.

New furniture designs, adaptations of traditional styles, reproductions, and new materials and finishes all contribute to the endless array of choices. The importation of many new and interesting products, with ethnic and global influences and creative and innovative qualities, allows the imagination to soar and results to dazzle.

Fabrics and Finishes

The textile industry is currently one area of great innovation. Because of continued research and new applications for textiles, our choices and their range of design and dependability have increased tremendously in the past few years. High-tech fibers and fabrics have created many new uses for textiles in residential design.

In the same vein, finishes have undergone a revolution as well. Improvements in the reliability and safety of these products, and a decrease in their environmental damage, have also given the designer better choices for design projects.

Investment versus Trendy

Designers have to rely on their education, experience, and talent to continually evaluate current design trends. Fashion can change quickly and it can be fickle, but good design is never outdated. When a client invests a great deal of money in a project, it is best to make choices based on good-quality design rather than on marketplace popularity.

FIGURE 2.17 Solar panels are an important interior as well as exterior feature of this home.

Responsibility and the Residential Designer

Our concepts and expectations of home are always changing—our wants become needs; the technological revolution affects us; we want our homes to run themselves; and new materials and finishes profoundly affect building practices as well as the number and quality of our choices. Residential designers need to keep abreast of all these changes by informing and educating themselves and staying ahead of the client. Clients are now more knowledgeable due to the proliferation of information on the Internet, advertisements, and design programs on television. For all these reasons, designers have increased responsibilities—to society, to our clients, to ourselves, and to the future health of our environment.

THE ERA OF ENVIRONMENTAL AWARENESS

As fellow occupants of this earth, we are witnessing and embracing a groundswell of interest and concern over the protection of our environment. What used to be the concern of only a small percentage of people has now become the topic of choice in all settings. Manufacturers, researchers, politicians, scientists, designers, architects, and the general public are now assuming roles in the fight to preserve and protect our fragile environment. Our concern affects our priorities and housing choices. Along the horizon we see the building of smaller houses, less urban sprawl, **gentrification** of our inner cities, adaptive uses, renovations, mandatory and more efficient recycling, and the continued search for solutions to our environmental problems.

It is the role of the residential designer to educate the public regarding choices that they can make to further this environmental cause. There are many alternative materials and finishes that are not as toxic to our environment or to the indoor air quality of homes. We have not only polluted the air outside of our houses but the air on the inside as well. In many cases, the indoor air quality is even worse than it is outside. The old phrase "go outside to get some fresh air" has become all too true.

The **site orientation** of our houses; the direction of our houses; the placement of windows and doors; and the use of **solar energy, HVAC (heating, ventilation, and air-conditioning) systems**, and certain types of building materials and insulation all contribute to energy consumption. If we can change our attitudes and habits, then we can change our building preferences and contribute in a positive way. Residential designers have the responsibility to educate, promote, and implement ways to reduce the negative impact home-building can have on the environment.

CULTURAL ENRICHMENT

Residential designers need to appreciate and respect the cultural differences of many of their clients. The differences and unique qualities of everyone involved make the profession of design so rewarding and interesting. We encounter and work closely with people of different generations and cultural backgrounds, with individual and varying tastes. In addition to accommodating the different needs and expectations of these diverse groups, the importation of many new products has definitely affected the quantity and quality of our choices. Designers are influenced and inspired by the creations of other cultures. The explosion in accessibility of the world markets has given us an infinite number of sources to stimulate our imagination and heighten our creative senses.

The Residential Designer as Facilitator

The role of the residential designer is to help the client reach his or her housing goals. Many of us know what we want in a home, but we do not always know how to achieve the desired results. The world of home buying, building, renovating, and designing can be overwhelming and ever-changing. What is old can become new and what is new can become old very quickly. New technology, adaptive uses, revolutionary materials and finishes, codes, costs, and availability can almost make the average homeowner want to order the finished and furnished home out of the 1908 Sears catalog, simply by selecting choice A, B, C, or D. (The first catalog actually had 44 choices.)

The designer can facilitate this process by close and direct involvement with the client as a result of years of study and continued education, experience, imagination, and creativity. The designer can enable, encourage, and assist the clients in finding solutions to his or her unique housing problems. The designer can help define needs, suggest improvements, or do the planning as the residence rises, block by block, board by board, from the ground up.

CAREER TIP

Every person in a residence could have different likes and dislikes. With the numerous products available, there is something for everyone. The project's continuity might take more effort on the part of the interior designer, but digging a little deeper will enhance the end result.

SUMMARY

A career as a residential designer involves knowing the history of design, architecture past and present, art, the new and ever-changing styles and materials, new technology and how it relates to our homes, and changing personal preferences. The list may go on and on, but it keeps the field of residential design dynamic and fascinating.

Interior Designer Profile 2.1: Marilyn Raines, Final Touch Interiors, Springfield, Missouri

Marilyn is a very successful business owner. She has been in business for 36 years, almost 25 of which have been in interior design. Having studied at Missouri State University, Raines is a member of ASID, a past president of Springfield Design Association, and a board member of the Missouri Coalition for Interior Design. She is also a past president of the Missouri East Chapter of ASID, St. Louis, and has received many local awards and citations.

Raines offers the following insight into her career:

- Begin your career with education and then work with a designer to get experience.
- Learn to "work" at interior design. You need to love the business.
- Quickly learn to participate in projects, ask questions, get involved, and don't stand back.
- Begin a residential project with an extensive interview, listen to what the client wants, and ask leading questions.
- Develop good relationships with clients to ensure repeat business. Those relationships are the true rewards of the interior design profession. Clients add another quality dimension to your life.
- Clients are more knowledgeable today due to the media and the Internet. Some clients are overwhelmed with all the information and options. Have clients bring in pictures of what they like or what they may have in mind.
- A fragile economy does affect residential design, with some clients choosing to remodel rather than build a new home.
- All interior designers virtually have their own business, especially with residential design. You have your own clients, one-on-one, even when you work with other designers in a large business.

RELATED CAREER OPTIONS

ADA Specialist

Architectural Space Planner

Art and Accessories Dealer

Antiques Dealer

Author

AutoCAD Specialist

Bedding Designer

Carpet and Flooring Designer

Children's Spaces Designer

Construction Firm Owner

Custom Framer

Custom Window Treatment Specialist

Design Consultant

Energy Conservationist

Environmental Designer

Faux Finisher

Feng Shui Specialist

Fireplace Designer

Floral Designer

Furniture Designer

Furniture Restorator

Furniture Retail Salesperson

Green Designer

Kitchen and Bath Designer

Landscape Designer

Loft Specialist

Manufactured Housing Specialist

Outdoor Living Designer

Paint Manufacturer

Real Estate Broker

Renderer

Residential Consultant

Space Planner

Staging Specialist

Stairway Designer

Trend Forecaster

Universal Designer

Upholsterer

SKILLS AND APTITUDES The residential designer needs to: Communicate well with clients.• Have a warm and friendly personality. • Be a good listener. • Be flexible. • Have the ability to work in a group. •Be a mediator and a facilitator. • Be able to create visuals for the client. • Be proficient with the computer. • Be knowledgeable of all the aspects pertaining to residential design.

EDUCATION A bachelor degree in interior design is preferred, but an associate degree as well as a certificate or other diploma program provides a good foundation when pursuing a career in residential interior design. There is so much that a designer (or decorator, depending on education) can be responsible for that the highest level of education possible should be the goal. Your confidence and credibility increase with your level of education. Many colleges and universities have master's degree programs and a few have PhD programs. With a master's degree, and especially a PhD, teaching becomes an option—another valuable and rewarding career.

KEY TERMS

- Aesthetics
- Americans with Disabilities Act (ADA)
- Demographics
- Design Concept
- Design Elements
- Design Principles
- Design Psychology
- Environmental Design
- Gentrification
- HVAC (Heating, Ventilation, and Air-Conditioning) Systems
- IRC (International Residential Codes)
- Private Spaces
- Programming
- Public Spaces
- Retrofit
- Site Orientation
- Solar Energy
- Sustainability
- Universal Design

DISCUSSION QUESTIONS

1. Discuss the relevance of psychology and sociology to interior design.
2. Discuss the importance of being licensed in interior design and how it might affect your career.
3. Discuss the personal rewards of being an interior designer.

CHAPTER THREE
COMMERCIAL INTERIORS

3

CHAPTER OBJECTIVES

Identify commercial interior design projects. • Understand the **code** requirements necessary for designing commercial spaces. • Understand the use and importance of psychology in commercial environments. • Understand the commercial interior design project **client**. Know what types of professionals, and how many, will work together to complete a commercial interior space. • Understand the ways to make money as a commercial interior designer. • Recognize potential trouble areas when designing commercial interiors. Determine the professional liabilities related to a commercial interior design project. Know when a commercial interior design project is complete.

Commercial spaces are specifically designed for their function. Types of commercial interiors include: corporate, healthcare, hospitality, restaurant, and educational. Commercial interior design requires additional attention to professional education, and in most states, licensing or state registration is also necessary. In order to be licensed or registered, interior designers are required to have passed the **National Council for Interior Design Qualification (NCIDQ)** exam.

Code Requirements

Professional interior designers must be well-informed about requirements and **building codes** for building interiors in order to ensure the health, safety, and welfare of those who occupy their spaces. Functionality followed by aesthetics is the rule when shaping the design of an interior space. After considering materials in light of requirements and codes, design decisions may be adjusted or totally changed. Budget restrictions can also dramatically alter the design.

Being aware of building codes, regulations, and budgetary requirements on a project will save time, money, and aesthetic integrity. Redesigning specific areas or changing selections without redesigning the entire project can be a difficult and time-consuming interior design challenge, especially if changes occur while a job is in progress and products are already on order.

A checklist of code requirements is used at the beginning and the completion of each commercial project. The use of this checklist at the beginning ensures that appropriate products are specified. Additionally, this list allows corrections and changes to take place before they become liabilities. A checklist referred to as a **walk-through** near the completion of a project is part of the confirmation that is required for final payment.

Commercial interior design is an area that does not work well for the self-proclaimed interior decorator or self-proclaimed interior designer. Education is a critical foundation for successful, functional commercial interior designs. What truly prepares an individual for commercial design is the combination of education and experience. Awareness of the responsibility and liability of commercial work, knowledge of codes, and an understanding of the public's wants and needs are critical qualities of the commercial designer. Designers validate their ability in commercial design with education, experience, registration, and licensing.

Education can be obtained through a diploma program at a community college, an online program, an art and design school, or a four-year degree program at an accredited college or university. Students must learn how to communicate both verbally and visually. Design students learn to sketch and draw in order to provide technical drawings and renderings. They learn to create material boards, use computer-aided software, and make models, all in order to visually communicate with clients. Students learn about codes and the importance of regulations for public safety and product durability. They learn to read blueprints, how to negotiate with clients, and write contracts and schedules. Commercial design students learn to apply their knowledge to the designing of public spaces, such as clinics, hospitals, churches, schools, businesses, offices, manufacturing plants, museums, and shopping malls.

The materials and furnishings that go into commercial interiors are regulated by codes that differ from state to state. Research is a key element in selecting products that are used for commercial buildings. Depending on the type and the public use of a building, testing and **material standards** differ.

Fire-resistant standards, product certification, product maintenance, and the product testing standards are documents that need to be cataloged for each commercial interior design project. A government regulator for each state will have the most current requirements that need to be complied with.

Accompanying a professional commercial interior design project should be a materials binder. A **materials binder** includes information on all materials and finishes that are installed and used for the project. A complete **materials and finish schedule** should be included for easy reference. The materials binder can be an electronic document, a hard copy, or both.

CAREER TIP

Sometimes the years required for higher education can seem too many, the rewards too far away. We live in an impatient society. Consider what you are doing while you could be furthering your education. Time flies! Be the best you can be in your profession.

This information will assist in the day-to-day building maintenance, insurance, and any questions regarding the performance of any installed product or material. The information is also useful for adding additional products or materials and for building additions.

The **Americans with Disabilities Act (ADA)** is the standard of regulation for commercial buildings. States differ in their standard requirements and testing, but ADA is the overriding regulation for everyone. This federal law requires that all commercial and public accommodations be accessible to people with disabilities. Interior designers are responsible for designing interior spaces that conform to these requirements.

Barrier-free design is required for commercial interiors and should be required for residential interiors but is not always considered, depending on the buildings and individuals involved. Some of the many facilities and products that barrier-free design addresses are: ramps, stairs, doorways, plumbing fixtures, floor surfaces, appliances, furnishings, signage, and alarms.

FIGURE 3.1 Barrier-free design is necessary for public spaces.

Universal design is a term that is used for design that meets the needs of all people, regardless of age or disability. With the universal design concept, spaces are not divided according to special needs. Designing spaces that work for most types of people is the concept. An example of universal design promotes aging in place as opposed to moving the aged into special age-related facilities. A universal design for a building would be designed with only one type of entrance instead of steps in one area and a ramp in another area.

A commercial interior designer needs to keep informed regarding ADA, accessible and barrier-free design, and universal design. Specializing in these specific types of interior design has widened the job market.

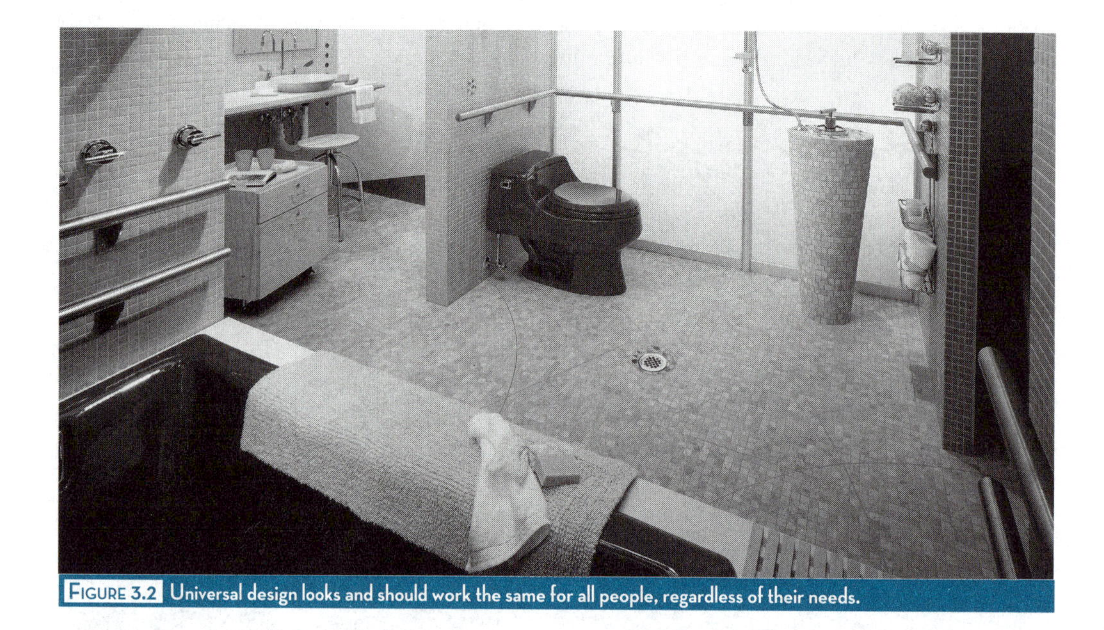

FIGURE 3.2 Universal design looks and should work the same for all people, regardless of their needs.

Psychology in Commercial Environments

Environmental psychology is an integral part of planning commercial interiors. People who use commercial space have a variety of needs and expectations that should be addressed by the interior designer. When a person enters a building, what does he or she expect? Interior space expectations are not necessarily conscious expectations.

Is the environment for product sales? What is being sold and to what type of client? Is the environment for service transactions? What service is being offered and to what group of people?

Environmental psychology is an area of expertise that is extremely important in planning commercial interiors. Psychology of interior design can easily be a specialized business. Aspects of interior design psychology such as color forecasting, for example, or the effects of color, public color preference, or current trends all make this an exciting and significant career.

COLOR PSYCHOLOGY IN THE COMMERCIAL ENVIRONMENT

Color plays a major role in environmental psychology. **Colorists** are available to assist interior designers in planning spaces for special needs. The psychology of color is a very in-depth study. Understanding basic psychology and color theory can contribute to our awareness of how color can affect a person—which emotional reactions that can take place based on color in a space. Educated interior designers have the basic knowledge of color psychology required to create environments that are comfortable and pleasing for the general public. Designers select colors based on the type of commercial situation and the activities that are going to take place in the space.

Designers who specialize in restaurant and hospitality use color to their advantage to affect the way food looks. Warm colors such as red, yellow, and orange are happy. These colors are great for food consumption and food sales. Studies show that a person's saliva glands are more active and food digests more easily when surrounded by warm colors. Restaurants, cafeterias, and kitchen areas are most successfully designed using these colors.

FIGURE 3.3 This artwork of oversized fruits and vegetables introduce a unique look for dining.

Warm colors can be exciting and playful. They are especially helpful when enhancing children's areas. Yellow is a sunshine color. Bright colors in any hue can create a very cheerful environment. Designers working with childcare environments, schools, or play areas in hospitals can create happy and cheerful spaces for children.

FIGURE 3.4 Well-supervised is the key to a children's play area within an office.

Cool colors such as blue, green, and purple are more calming and relaxing. Interior designers should carefully consider the use of purple because it can become violent or depressing depending on the color value or shade. Purples work well in funeral homes. Blues and greens are great for areas where the clientele might be uptight for any reason. Blues and greens work well in healthcare waiting areas. Interior designers who specialize in these areas do best, from a psychological perspective, when they select from the appropriate palette.

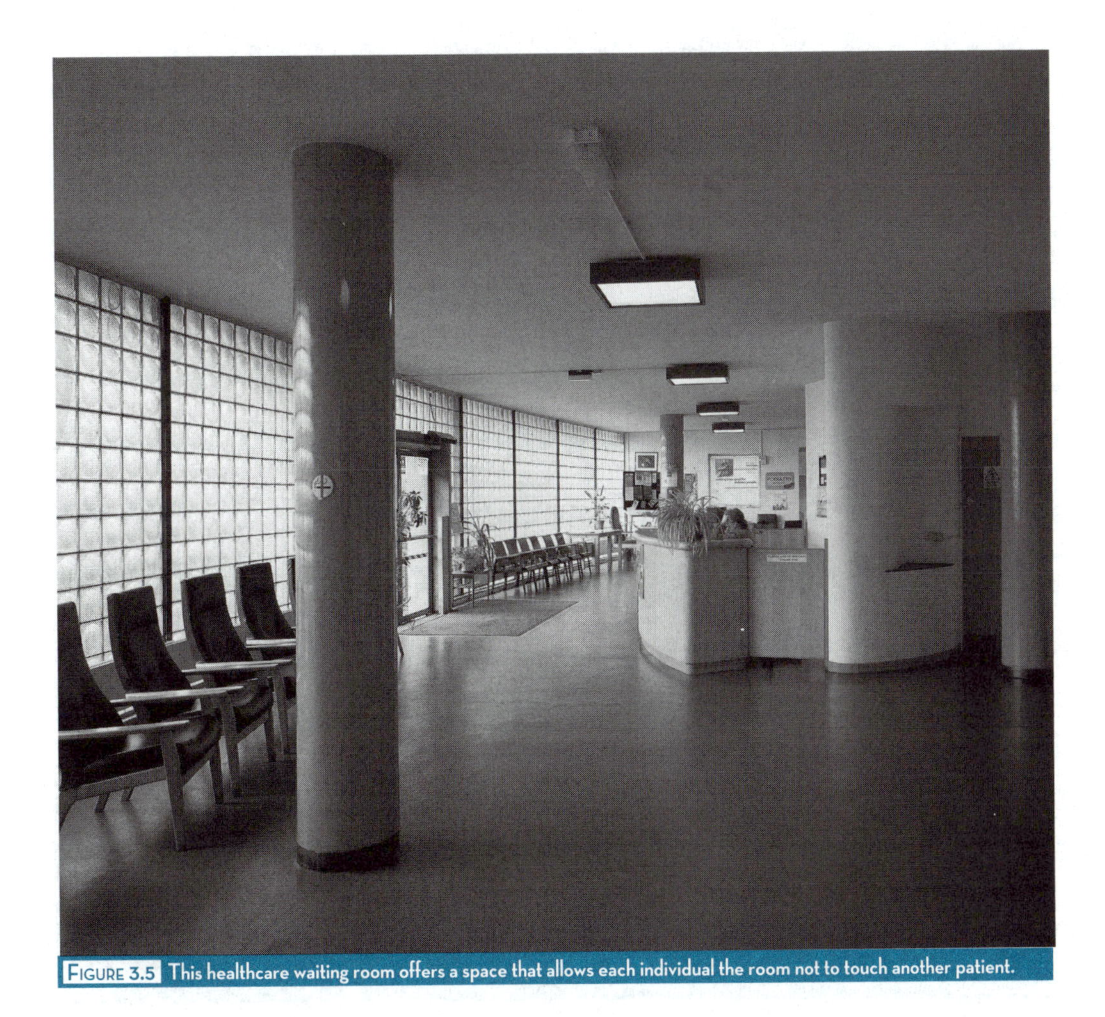

FIGURE 3.5 This healthcare waiting room offers a space that allows each individual the room not to touch another patient.

Pink has been shown to calm aggressive behavior. Because we associate pink with softness, it has been used in prisons and jails to calm aggressive feelings and behavior.

Gray is great for presentations. Gray is a strong color and creates a nice backdrop for numerous types of presentations, displays, or people. Complementary colors create a relaxing viewing environment and are thus helpful under special conditions. This allows a person to have a more restful working environment. Designers who work with corporate offices, general office spaces, or product showrooms can help clients select colors to enhance and promote their products.

FIGURE 3.6 This creative presentation room enhances creative thinking.

A hospital operating room is a good example of the use of complementary colors. Operating rooms should be a shade of green, which is the complement of red. The green environment will help a physician who is working with blood (or the color red) to not only see the red better but also to stave off fatigue. Designers who specialize in healthcare study color and how it can enhance the health and well-being of patients and medical practices in general.

Other complementary combinations are yellow and purple, and orange and blue. These complementary color combinations work well in general office areas where many computers are used. A good example would be a call center for telemarketing.

FIGURE 3.7 This color scheme offers a dramatic contrast of color. (See color plate 4.)

Theater colors should be rich jewel tones that emphasize the dramatic environment. A library, on the other hand, should be a deep and restful color, such as forest green, deep blue, or dark purple. These colors are conducive to quiet reading or studying. Along with restful colors, quiet materials like carpet should be considered. Soft materials are also great to mix with the hard surfaces of tables and bookshelves. An acoustical consideration of the interior surfaces provides a better functioning library environment.

FIGURE 3.8 A soft and quiet color scheme is conducive for study in this school library. (See color plate 5.)

School corridors and school public spaces are ideal for specific school colors that can also reflect school spirit. In the classroom, the front of the room or **headwall** should be a medium to dark color of blue or green. This will help keep student attention to the front of the room. These colors are also less tiresome for the student. The remainder of the classroom should be a neutral color like beige.

FIGURE 3.9 A contrasting headwall draws the student's attention to the front of the room. (See color plate 6.)

FIGURE 3.10 Dramatic jewel tones are perfect for this school auditorium. (See color plate 7.)

OTHER AREAS OF PSYCHOLOGY AND COMMERCIAL INTERIOR DESIGN

Environmental psychology is also about the selection and placement of materials and furnishings. Floor coverings, wall coverings, furniture, and accessories can create a mood that is casual, formal, rugged, or refined. All interior finishes and furnishings should define the type of commercial interior and its intended use.

Appropriate selection of materials is crucial because of the various effects of those materials in different settings; the tactile qualities, pattern, color, and even the acoustical properties have to be evaluated. Designers use the weight and positioning of interior materials to enhance sound control, in addition to considering the acoustical and textural properties of many textiles.

Seating, for example, is specific in each commercial space. Airports, doctors' offices, restaurants (both formal and casual), banks, spas, and nightclubs all require seating. All of these areas have seating needs and all of them require a different type of seating for their respective functions.

Interior designers are increasingly planning individual, private, small, and open seating areas that are both inside and outdoors at commercial workplaces. These small gathering spaces are meeting the needs of workers who are confined to **cubicle** workstations. These spaces are also a solution for office conferences that do not require a private conference room.

FIGURE 3.11 This office interior encourages a healthy working environment.

FIGURE 3.12 This space offers a pleasant relief from the working space.

Strangers do not like to touch each other when seated in close proximity. Interior designers need to recognize personal space. The study of how people relate to space and the people in it has provided verifiable information regarding this sociological phenomenon. **Proxemics** takes cultural differences into consideration. Some groups do not mind sharing small spaces with others, while some prefer keeping strangers at a distance. Arranging furniture accordingly is necessary for individual comfort. Chair arms, tables, plants, and lighting serve as dividers. Three-seat sofas usually only seat two people because the middle seat is too close for comfort. In hospital waiting areas, sofas are avoided because they turn into sleeping areas for the sleep-deprived family members of patients.

Seating in banks or a doctor's office should be secluded enough that another person's personal business is not overheard or read. **Family Educational Rights and Privacy Act (FERPA)** laws now mandate the division of private conversation spaces for the general public. Interior designers are faced with the challenge of dividing space without sacrificing the integrity of the design or the privacy of the public. Designers need to strike a balance in creating private areas while avoiding confinement and isolation, especially in sometimes very tense medical or business situations.

FIGURE 3.13 This very friendly bank lobby offers hospitality and privacy for all customers.

FIGURE 3.14 Hospital waiting areas usually provide larger spaces for patient division.

FIGURE 3.15 This general office waiting area looks very much like a living room.

The way that spaces within a commercial interior are divided can dictate how the public perceives the environment. A clear glass door as opposed to an opaque one, whether of frosted glass or some other material, shows that nothing is hiding on the other side. Yet a solid wood, metal, or even frosted glass door can helpfully separate a private space from the public. Having an opening with no door allows the public to travel easily between spaces both physically and visually. Designers who focus on space planning analyze the intended traffic patterns and circulation needs, and devise ways to move the public in an efficient, safe, and plainly marked direction.

Most everyone has had the experience of arriving to an appointment and being greeted by a person behind a small, uninviting window. This is not an acceptable design detail for an office that desires a friendly image. Office space needs to reflect the type of product or service that is being offered.

A professional office needs to look like professionals work there. The same concept is true with any business. The interior design should reflect the specific service being offered.

FIGURE 3.16 This Harley-Davidson office projects its brand-name product information.

FIGURE 3.17 Bass Pro corporate offices have numerous custom details showing their "Bass Pro look."

Who Is Your Client?

Your client is the decision-maker. On a new building project, the person or persons who own the building are usually the client. On an existing building, sometimes a purchasing agent is the decision-maker. Sometimes the chief executive officer or the chief financial officer is the decision-maker. It is extremely important that the interior designer work with the person in charge of approving the interior design decisions.

Letters of agreement are important before beginning any project. Good business principles are a must. If signatures are not acquired, work should not begin. Using **retainer fees**, or **down payments**, are a good business practice. Letters of agreement, like contracts, spell out in detail the scope of the project, all services to be performed, and all payment information. Templates for letters of agreement are available from many sources, such as **ASID**. A letter of agreement can be written by the interior designer, an attorney, or any of the participants.

Who Makes Up the Team of Professionals?

The business owner is the team leader on a new building project or on the renovation of an existing building. A balanced professional team includes: an architect, engineer, interior designer, general contractor, plumber, heating and air-conditioning expert, electrician, and numerous other **subcontractors**. Some of the subcontractors might be experts in: ceilings, lighting, flooring, walls, furnishings, windows and doors, **millwork**, window treatments, hardware, audio, alarms, music, the Internet, televisions, phones, **white noise**, and safety features such as smoke alarms, sprinkler systems, and exit lighting.

Even though the final decision-makers are the clients, the architects and interior designers are usually the contact people who communicate directly with the client. If the interior designer works for the architectural firm, the architect is the person who communicates with the owner. If the interior designer works independently from the architect, the interior designer also reports directly to the business owner. The interior designer and the architect need to communicate well with each other regardless of whom they are working for.

On commercial buildings, it is very important that all professionals, contractors, and subcontractors communicate often and clearly with all team members. In addition to frequent face-to-face meetings, e-mail is a wonderful communication tool. Recording transactions and all communication is very important to the success of a project. When everything is written, there are fewer mistakes and miscommunications. It is also important to date all communication. Dates are necessary for hard copies of any documentation.

CAREER TIP

Networking with professionals will enhance your career.

Ways to Make Money in Commercial Interior Design

Hourly fees for interior designers vary depending on the number of designers working on a project and the experience level of each interior designer. Interior design fees are charged very much like services in other professions. Designer levels include: secretarial, computer-aided drawing and design (CADD),

intern designer, junior designer, senior designer, rendering artist, and project manager.

Services are billed at different rates depending on the skill and experience level of each professional. In addition to hourly interior design services, clients are charged for expenses such as gas mileage, phone charges, fax charges, plotting expenses, and sample costs. Accurate bookkeeping is extremely important in maintaining a profitable interior design business. Expenses can easily be forgotten and not billed with multiple projects and busy schedules.

It is common for an interior designer who works alone to charge one hourly fee regardless of the service provided. In this case, services are also recorded carefully for the same accurate bookkeeping. Commercial interior designers who work alone are typically senior-level professionals with years of experience.

Product sales are also a profit center for interior designers. Interior designers sell paint, wall coverings, window treatments, furniture, and accessories. These can be sold in several ways: retail, a percentage off of retail, **cost-plus,** or at cost. The **profit margin** on products sold is sometimes related to the hourly interior design fees that are charged.

Selling furniture is a career that some commercial interior designers enjoy and profit from. Major office furniture manufacturers distribute their products through limited dealerships. Each manufacturer limits its distribution to one or two dealers per city, depending on the size of the market area. A **sales representative** makes the necessary contacts and promotes the products.

Each major furniture manufacturer distributes products to selected area dealers to compete in each market area. Within each market area, **bidding** on commercial furnishings is a standard way for business owners to get the best price for interior products.

Sometimes the profit margins on products are not discussed with clients. This is seldom the case in commercial interior design, which has higher dollar volumes and usually more competition for the sale of products. Some companies will forgo the interior design hourly fee in exchange for product sales.

Interior designers are in a position to sell the products, oversee the purchasing, or both. Planning interior spaces around specific manufacturers' products is a common career path for commercial interior designers. Many times, commercial interior designers work as a team or as an individual for a company whose interest is in the profit from furniture sales and installation.

CAREER TIP

In a Yahoo! Education online article "Six Flexible Careers That Pay $70K," Gabby Hyman wrote, "Interior designers also lead the way in the number of self-employed, flexible career professionals with 26 percent running their own companies/consultancies. Train for the field through an associate degree program, but add a bachelor's degree in art or design to advance to the more flexible positions. Study fabrics, CAD design, ergonomics, color theory, and more. The top 50 percent in the field earned on average between $60,200 and $81,800 in 2007."

Commissions for product sales can also be a profit center. Commissions are paid to interior designers by companies that provide products directly to the client. Commissions are also paid to the interior designer from dealers who successfully get business as a result of the interior designer's specifications.

Commercial interior designers also charge by the **square foot**. This is profitable with large buildings, repeated designs, and large open spaces. Interior designers who work with primarily large facilities profitably charge this way. Square foot pricing is easy to calculate and has fewer bookkeeping items to keep track of. A percentage of the total amount for a project is billed when that percentage of the job is complete.

Charging a **fixed fee** for a commercial interior design project is another common way to make money. A fixed fee is typically arrived at by the interior designer reviewing the scope of services and estimating the amount of time and energy that will be necessary to complete the job. Using this method, the interior design firm charges percentages of the fixed fee at specified time lines.

Potential Trouble Areas

Communication and careful supervision of the interior design specifications are required to ensure a successful project. Being available to answer questions as they arise will alleviate potential problems resulting from misinterpretations. Interior designers can be guilty of assuming they are clearly understood by all subcontractors or clients. Interior design details need to be clearly communicated through drawings, sketches, and written instructions.

On occasion, the relationship between the professional and the client can become strained. Good communication is vital. Sometimes problems can occur between the architect and contractor or contractor and subcontractors, etc. The interior designer can become the mediator in many cases. Regardless of the situation, problems need to be solved in order for the project to run smoothly.

Commercial interior designers work closely with architects in space planning for maximum functioning in the interior environment. Furniture and fixture placement should be considered along with the door and window locations. When planning a new building that will utilize existing furnishings, careful consideration is necessary for the placement of all items to be reused.

When interior designers are not consulted until the structural plans are complete, changes are usually required. These **change orders** are very expensive for the client. Doors, windows, heating and air-conditioning vents, and lighting locations are extremely important in planning the interior design.

Partial shipments or products that are shipped from more than one **dye lot** create problems with incomplete installations or colors that do not match. Damaged shipments can also create lengthy delays while waiting for new merchandise.

Industry **strikes** can cause delays in entire projects. Examples of these are steel, trucking, and any area where **unions** are involved. Each part of a new building is connected to the whole. New construction usually experiences numerous delays in product delivery. Unpredictable weather conditions also cause project delays.

At the beginning of a new project, it is helpful to discuss some of the potential trouble areas that are out of your control. And it is impossible to guess what the unexpected situations might be. Stressing patience and allowing a realistic amount of time is extremely helpful in maintaining client satisfaction.

Professional Liabilities

Liability insurance is available for interior designers. Liability insurance protects the designer in case of faulty products, if a costly mistake is made, or if someone is hurt as a result of something he or she has specified, in addition to other reasons a designer might get sued. One type of liability insurance is labeled **errors and omissions insurance**. Interior design organizations such as ASID and IIDA have professional insurance available for their membership, for those interested in purchasing it.

The basis for most liability lawsuits are **misrepresentation**, **breach of contract, implied warranty of fitness, professional negligence, joint and several liability,** and **liability without fault for design defects.** Liability suits most likely take place when an interior designer has liability insurance. When a client knows the designer has insurance, they're more likely to sue.

To protect against possible liability suits, interior designers can: perform within their area of expertise, use contracts and specifications, know and comply with codes and regulations, use reputable contractors, keep accurate records, and spend enough time supervising.

Product liabilities are turned over to the manufacturer who supplied the product in question. Each year the **U.S. Consumer Product Safety Commission** publishes a list of product-related accidents. Many state statutes allow product-related claims to be filed against a manufacturer when an injury occurs, regardless of the age or condition of the product in question.

When Is the Interior Design Project Complete?

The interior design project is complete when all contracted work is finished. The walk-through and **punch list** are signed. Clients should express approval and have all appropriate papers signed and money paid for all products and services. Interior designers should ask clients to discuss their favorite details of the project. Interior designers should let clients know what they like best about the job as well. Each job provides more experience for the designer and that increases the knowledge base.

"Satisfactory" is a term that is helpful with contracts for both products and services. Occasionally, there is a small detail that requires waiting for a part or extra service work. When this happens, satisfactory completion is noted so the process of finishing payment can be finalized. Good professionals will ensure that the small details are completed as soon as possible.

Interior designers spend a lot of time with clients. Great friendships evolve from good business relationships. It is appropriate to maintain these friendships. Over a number of years, repeat business is important. A job well done and a lasting client/designer friendship is one very important key to a successful, growing, interior design business. These friendships are also one of the most fulfilling and rewarding aspects of the job.

Interior Designer Profile 3.1
Vickie Stewart, Past President, Missouri West/Kansas ASID

An interior designer for 32 years, Vickie Stewart has reached the pinnacle of her profession not only through her hard work, talent, and reputation but through her involvement in the community and her affiliations, which include her role as president of the Missouri West/Kansas chapter of ASID, where she also served as treasurer and chapter secretary. She has served as co-chair for the ASID Designer Showhouse, is a professional member of IIDA, and is a member of the Commercial Brokers Association (CBA) and Commercial Real Estate Women (CREW). Stewart is currently director of interior design for Rosemann & Associates, P.C., an architectural, interior design, structural engineering, and planning firm. Rosemann & Associates specializes in multifamily housing, senior living, military housing, student housing, historic renovation, condominiums, lofts, and commercial and boutique hotels.Stewart received her BS in interior design from the University of Missouri-Columbia.

"Over the course of my 32 years in the profession of interior design," Stewart says, "I have done both residential and commercial design and I prefer commercial. Due to the 'business' nature of the commercial interior design project, I am exposed to the level of professionalism that I enjoy. I enjoy the 'business of interior design' and my current job gives me the opportunity to work in that environment. Contracts, codes, budgets, committees, [and] finances are all areas that challenge me on a daily basis. While I still am allowed a creative outlet, I am allowed to enjoy my craft set amid the business background."

Her advice for students or professionals interested in commercial interiors? "Strengthen your business acumen by learning business strategies and their effect on a company's bottom line," she says. "Just like any excellent interior designer, you should develop the following skills:

Listening • Effective Communication (interior design terminology)
Psychology • Teamwork • Computer • Strategic Planning
Color Theory • Networking • Branding

"In this competitive marketplace, your skill set is what sets you apart from all the others so it is mandatory to continually be learning and growing professionally and personally. Anything you can do to enhance your professional persona and entrench yourself into the area of commercial interior design will be beneficial to your career path."

SUMMARY

The number of job opportunities and of different areas of design in the commercial segment is enormous. Many of the projects can take a considerable length of time and many people become involved. This creates an opportunity to meet many different allied professionals and build a large network of successful people who have a great deal in common and can share the ups and downs of these working situations.

Our commercial environments play a big role in **commerce**—in healthcare, for example, as the place to treat and house the sick; in schools, where our children spend their days; and in every other imaginable type of facility for every other type of commercial human need. The role of the designer is to create these spaces to be the best that they can be for all those who inhabit them.

RELATED CAREER OPTIONS

- Acoustic Designer
- ADA Specialist
- Adaptive Reuse Specialist
- Advertising Professional
- Architectural Space Planner
- Art and Accessories Dealer
- Buyer
- City Planner
- Civil Drafter
- Code Specialist
- Colorist
- Commercial Carpet and Flooring Designer
- Communication Designer
- Computer Software Engineer
- Construction Firm Professional
- Contract Designer
- Cost Estimator
- Designer for Photo Shoots
- Designer for Corporate Functions
- Display Window Designer
- Educational Facilities Designer
- Energy Conservationist
- Entertainment Facility Designer
- Environmental Designer
- Event Designer
- Exhibit Designer
- Facilities Manager
- Franchise Designer
- Funeral Designer
- Gallery Owner
- Graphic Designer
- Green Designer
- Historic Preservationist
- Hospitality Designer
- Industrial Designer
- In-house Commercial Designer
- Kitchen and Bath Designer
- Landscape Designer
- Lighting Specialist
- Loft Designer
- Mall Designer
- Manufacturers' Representative
- Market Researcher
- Merchandise Display Designer
- Model Creator
- Model Designer
- Nightclub Designer
- Office Systems Sales Representative
- Office Systems Specialist
- Packaging Designer
- Park Designer
- Project Manager
- Property Manager
- Publicist
- Real Estate Broker
- Religious Designer
- Restaurant Designer
- Retail Designer
- Sales Representative
- Salon Designer
- Set Designer
- Showroom Designer
- Spa Designer
- Space Planner
- Textile Designer
- Tile Designer
- Universal Designer
- Visual Merchandiser
- Window Display Designer

SKILLS AND APTITUDES There are many skills and aptitudes that benefit the commercial designer. Understanding the public and its needs and preferences in general guide some of the choices that the designer makes. Of course, you can't please everyone, but the more you know, the better you will serve the clients, whomever they may be. Being able to work with large numbers of people, flexibility, diplomacy, and being a skilled mediator are valuable assets. Being a good communicator and being organized, thorough, and attentive is also very important. A successful commercial designer needs to be an excellent collaborator yet confident in making decisions and taking the lead when appropriate. Attention to detail, tracking and documenting all progress, being vigilant concerning codes, and constantly keeping up with new and improved materials and applications are also key. Expertise in business can be particularly helpful since many commercial projects involve business, at least on some level. But most important, you need to love what you do—when you do, it is contagious.

KEY TERMS

- Americans with Disabilities Act (ADA)
- ASID
- Barrier-Free Design
- Bidding
- Breach of Contract
- Building Codes
- Change Order
- Client
- Code
- Colorist
- Commerce
- Commissions
- Cost-Plus
- Cubicle
- Down Payment
- Dye Lot
- Errors and Omissions Insurance
- Family Educational Rights and Privacy Act (FERPA)
- Fire-Resistant
- Fixed Fee
- Headwall
- Hourly Fee
- Implied Warranty of Fitness
- Intern Designer
- Joint and Several Liability
- Junior Designer
- Letter of Agreement
- Liability Without Fault for Design Defects
- Materials Binder
- Materials and Finish Schedule
- Material Standards
- Millwork
- Misrepresentation
- NCIDQ (National Council for Interior Design Qualification)
- Product Liability
- Product Sales
- Professional Negligence
- Profit Margin
- Proxemics
- Punch List
- Retainer Fee
- Sales Representative
- Satisfactory
- Senior Designer
- Square Foot
- Strike
- Subcontractor
- Union
- Universal Design
- U.S. Consumer Product Safety Commission
- Walk-Through
- White Noise

DISCUSSION QUESTIONS

1. Compare and contrast commercial and residential interior design.
2. Discuss the ways in which the design of commercial spaces can positively affect commerce, education, industry, recreational facilities, and other public needs.
3. Discuss the importance of being adept at working within a large group of professionals on one project. How can you better prepare yourself to work effectively and diplomatically within a professionally diverse group?

EDUCATION Formal education benefits a designer immensely. You can never receive too much. A bachelor degree is a worthy goal. An associate degree is beneficial as well; many students then go on to complete a bachelor degree. Other diploma programs can give you a foundation for decorating. Special certification in LEED (or any other specialized area) offers additional educational benefits.

Get as much experience as you can in all areas: business, retail, design firms, architectural firms, educational settings, manufacturing, or any situation where you can be involved in a commercial setting. Experience can begin while still in college through internships, job shadowing, and part-time jobs in any related field. Working with the public on any level can be insightful.

Education paired with experience will help you pass the NCIDQ exam; then the career ladder won't seem as steep and you can get to the top faster.

CHAPTER FOUR
HEALTHCARE

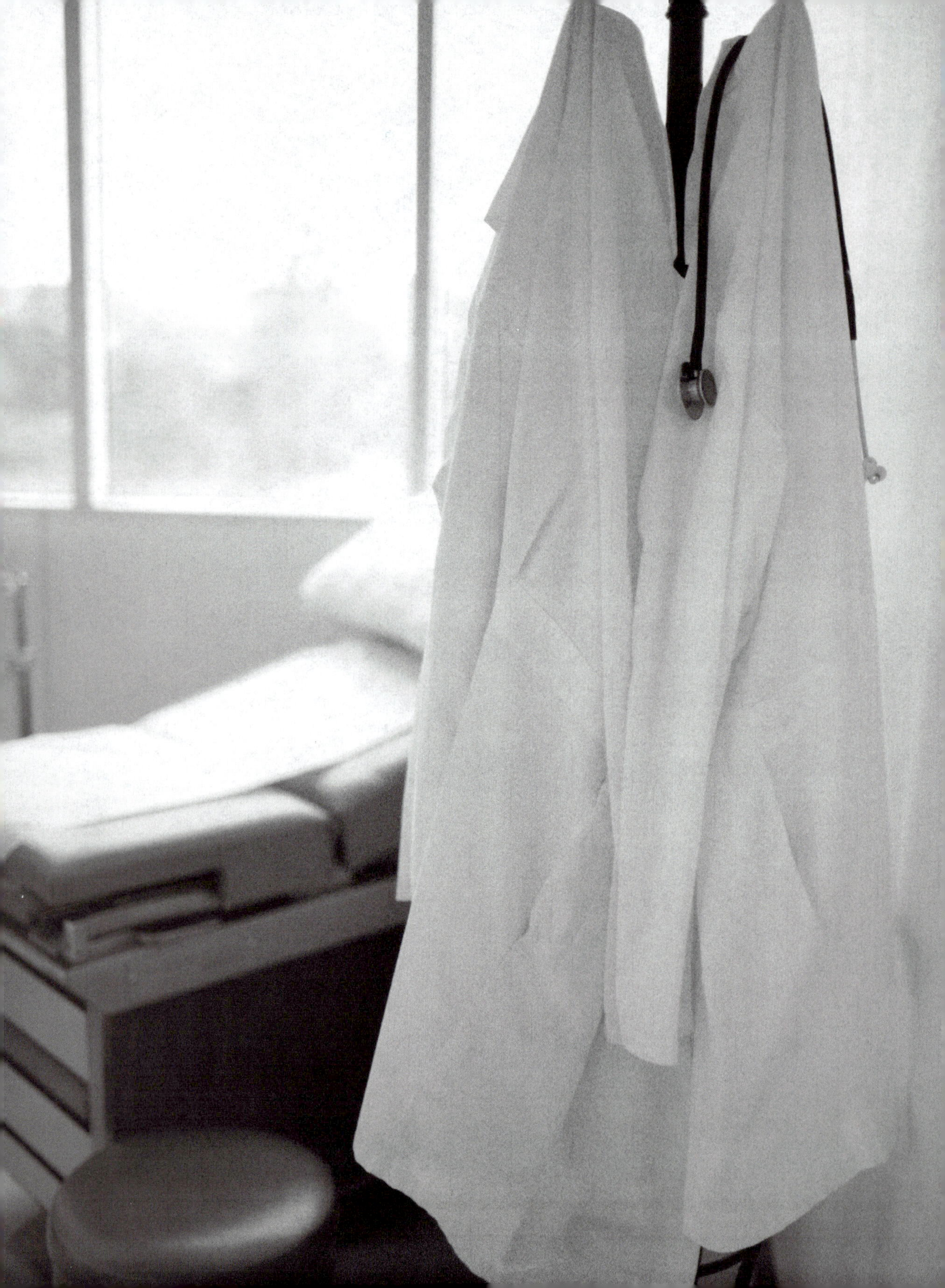

CHAPTER OBJECTIVES

After reading this chapter, you should understand how interior design applies to the wide range of healthcare facilities, including: Hospitals • Extended Care • Nursing Homes Assisted Living • Health Clinics • Physician Offices • Dental Offices Rehabilitation and Fitness Centers • Optometry Offices.

Design in healthcare has tremendous potential for the interior design practitioner. New and improved materials, cutting-edge technology, and an increase in specialized care are all on the rise along with ever-changing healthcare practices and regulations. It is critical that those involved in the design of healthcare facilities keep abreast of all these changes.

Interior designers who specialize in the healthcare industry work with extremely educated professionals. Time is a very important issue. Being punctual for appointments and being well-prepared will minimize the number of meetings necessary to get the interior design approved. Punctuality is always important, but with health issues that include life-and-death situations, sick patients waiting, and back-to-back appointments, healthcare personnel often have no time to spare. Productive and timely meetings with designers are crucial.

Interior designers can find many opportunities for specialization in certification or licensing in healthcare design. (This topic will be discussed in detail in Chapter Nine, "Certified Specialty Areas.")

The Family Educational Rights and Privacy Act (FERPA) requires some interior environment changes from previous designs. In healthcare facilities, private areas are necessary to preserve the patient's right for privacy. Reception areas and waiting rooms do not typically allow for private conversations so areas are set aside. It may be just a small room, visually and acoustically removed from the public areas, which allows for private conversation. Interior design and space planning that is very open has been rethought and reconfigured in the healthcare industry because of FERPA regulations. Reasons for privacy could include conversations about personal health, but also billing and other information exchanged in a healthcare setting. These private areas are designed to make patients and families more comfortable.

Interior designers can choose many specializations within the areas of healthcare, such as dental offices, working for healthcare furniture providers, laboratory design, and office filing and storage design. These are only a few of the many specific areas an interior designer might focus on in healthcare design. Interior design specialization can be as broad as the creative mind of the interior designer. There are neither bounds nor limits.

CAREER TIP

Limit the number of items that sick people handle and pass to others. An example would be toys for a child's waiting area. Consider DVDs for quiet viewing.

When working within the healthcare industry, be prepared. Know each healthcare facility and its functions. Know the procedures that are offered to patients. Understand what each procedure is called and what it entails.

There are many departments and many administrators involved when designing for healthcare. There must be a clear understanding of who makes the ultimate decision. In some cases it might be a committee or board of directors.

Clarity of purpose with interior design decisions will keep most employees satisfied and happy with their new environment. The interior design must be environmentally functional and safe for every area of healthcare. Space planning and circulation must promote employee efficiency. Ultimately, the design of the space should enhance patient care and comfort.

Healthcare in general requires the interior designer to listen carefully to the client and know as much as possible about the end user. Meeting the goals of the administration, budget, long-term planning, and codes and regulations all require consideration. The needs of the public, including the employees, patients, and guests, must all be examined in order to ensure the success of the facility.

There has been a great deal of research that either implies or proves that the interior design of healthcare spaces can have a positive impact on the patients' overall well-being and recovery. With this knowledge, much improvement has occurred in the aesthetics and the functionality of these spaces. Healthcare facilities are no longer institutional-white with harsh lighting.

CAREER TIP

If magazines are available to the public, they should not be more than three months old. Some healthcare providers consider magazine ads competition for money and services.

Healthcare Design for an Aging Population

As our population ages, health facilities evolve and increase in number. Healthcare is one of the primary areas where money is spent and is rarely an optional expenditure. Health facilities for our aging population include clinics, private practices, fitness centers, outpatient facilities, extended care, assisted care, and nursing homes. Several of these kinds of facilities will be discussed later in the chapter, but we must be cognizant of the fact that healthcare for our aging citizens constitutes a significant and growing proportion of the facilities required in our society today.

Hospitals

There are many types of hospitals. There are general hospitals and those that specialize in the care of children, burn victims, cancer patients, and cardiovascular diseases. Realizing the specific needs of each patient type is important within both specialty and general hospitals.

Hospitals address many types of needs: emergency care, waiting spaces, registration, pre-entrance screenings, food areas for guests and employees, gift shops, conference rooms, pharmacies, operating rooms, patient rooms, resting rooms for doctors, intensive care areas for numerous specific needs, administrative offices, and shipping and receiving areas for all of the above. Competition for consumers among healthcare facilities demands that the interior design for all areas not only be safe and functional but pleasant and environmentally healthy.

Eating areas with options are very important in hospitals. Twenty-four-hour cafeterias, restaurants, and snack and drink areas accommodate the continuous activity in a hospital. Hospitals are no different than other public-service buildings where food services are often leased to chain-food companies. The interior designer's job is to incorporate specific and separate corporate design into the overall hospital plan. This might mean creating a backdrop that would enhance someone else's design or a corporate logo. These eating spaces need to be comforting, efficient, clean, and aesthetically pleasing.

Hospital activity also includes public education. Conference and training rooms are included for scheduled events. Getting the general public to visit the hospital before a health need arises is a marketing advantage.

Hospital-auxiliary areas include general offices, purchasing areas, engineering spaces, maintenance and housekeeping areas, labs, kitchens, and an abundance of storage areas. These areas are integrated within the hospital for

CAREER TIP

White noise is extremely helpful in healthcare waiting areas because it provides a sense of calm and steadiness and enhances privacy for conversation and other personal sounds. Soft music delivered through sound systems can provide white noise in waiting areas of hospitals, doctors' offices, clinics, and even restaurants and other public areas. The music masks other sounds and brings a sense of relaxation when appropriately selected.

each function. Interior designers in healthcare must understand the total operations and the specific needs of each project.

Within the hospital structure there are also areas for long-term visitors, such as hotel rooms, that might be housed in a wing of the hospital. These specific hotel rentals are designed for visitors who prefer and need to be quickly accessible to a patient. Some guests also need to continue conducting business while attending to a loved one. A workspace with adequate room and lighting is important.

Restrooms and bathing areas for patients are becoming increasingly spa-like, with such comforts and amenities as warm towels, tubs with water jets, and soft lighting. Such features have become an expectation for patients, guests, and the general workforce alike. Well-designed restrooms make a noticeable difference and can be the competitive edge in the growing healthcare markets; everyone in any type of building uses restrooms. Designing them with flexibility, ease of cleaning, and trouble-free maintenance is critical. Restrooms need to be suitable for all ages, sizes, and shapes of people, including those with disabilities.

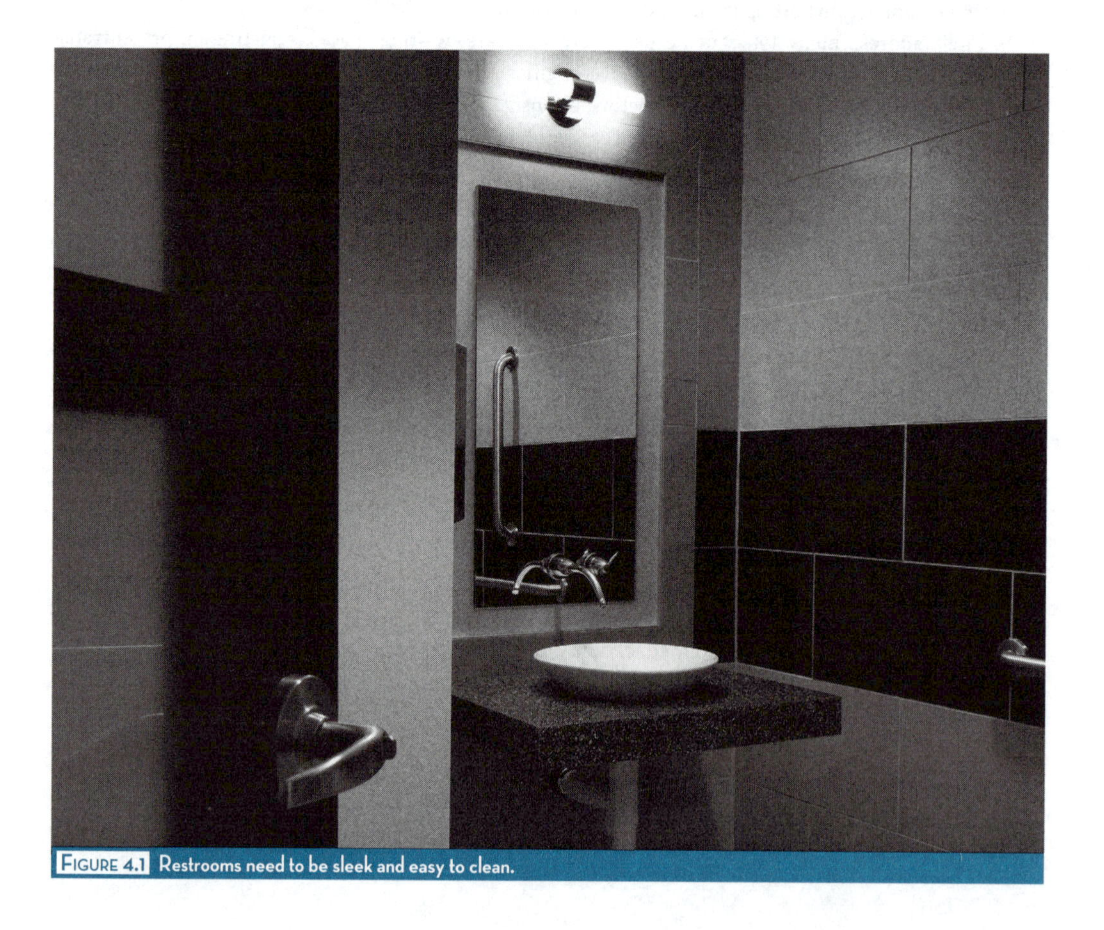

FIGURE 4.1 Restrooms need to be sleek and easy to clean.

FIGURE 4.2 Private restrooms in healthcare facilities do not have to feel institutional.

WAYFINDING AND HEALTHCARE

Wayfinding in hospitals is an interior design challenge. In any building that is large, the public needs to find their way around. Wayfinding must accommodate as many special-needs persons as possible. Thus, the interior designer should be aware of requirements for the old, the young, the color-blind, the seeing-impaired, the hearing-impaired, the mentally compromised, and all other people with special needs.

In addition to visuals, sounds and touch directions are important for wayfinding. Interior designers should incorporate at least three wayfinding methods for all areas in a healthcare structure. Handrails can incorporate touch and sound directions, water or music can direct with sounds, and color and patterns can direct visually.

The designer needs to be knowledgeable about sound, lighting, signage products, creative material usage for wayfinding, and the needs of those with various disabilities.

FIGURE 4.3 Themed art can depict specific healthcare areas.

FIGURE 4.4A & 4.4B Color can offer additional help with wayfinding. (See color plate 8.)

ENVIRONMENTAL PSYCHOLOGY

Healthcare involves many of life's most important events, both joyful and traumatic. Births, deaths, and every health-related concern happen in hospitals. The interior designer needs to know and work carefully with **environmental psychology.** Planning appropriate environments for individual areas that are both unique and have continuity with the entire building is important. Spaces appropriate for all health events must be allocated for: privacy, socializing, grieving, and shared happiness. Places for rest and to spend time waiting are needed.

FIGURE 4.5 A comfortable hospital waiting room.

FIGURE 4.6 Nonsterile approach to a waiting area.

Healthcare also encompasses a variety of stay lengths by patients, guests, and caregivers. Intensive-care waiting areas can turn into 24-hour waiting spaces or living areas. Interior designers must make appropriate selections to accommodate both comfort and durability.

Patient rooms have changed in recent years to be more user-friendly for the patient, the doctor, and guests. The traditional hospital room has a very new look. The hospital room is consistent with new medical technology. Both are more streamlined.

Outpatient procedures are more prevalent and require yet another type of hospital space. Outpatient areas are usually high-traffic, fast-paced, and compact. Very efficient traffic flow that progresses with medical functions enhances patient satisfaction. Moving smoothly from waiting rooms to check-in desks, to lab areas, and then to easily found examination rooms prevents patients from becoming too anxious. In many cases, specific rooms are hard to find and it is easy to get lost. When someone is not feeling well or is feeling rushed, simplifying the transition from one place to another is essential. Patients should not feel lost, pushed, or rushed.

FIGURE 4.7 Stylish yet relaxing waiting area.

FIGURE 4.8 The contemporary patient room is friendlier, with less of a traditional hospital look.

Extended Care

Many healthcare situations do not require constant hospital attention but do require extended nursing care. Sometimes after a serious illness or accident, patients are released from hospitals but are not able to totally care for themselves. Thus, extended-care facilities take over before patients go back to their home or to a nursing or long-term living and care situation.

Extended-care facilities can be freestanding residences, integrated spaces within a skilled nursing facility, part of a hospital, or components of a care/retirement community. These environments are usually more homelike in their interior design.

Nursing Homes

Nursing homes offer a higher level of care for those who do not require hospitalization but cannot care for themselves. Usually, the residents of a nursing home are elderly. To accommodate the needs of everyone, nursing homes should adapt to **universal design.**

Interior designers can make a significant difference in this highly competitive industry by offering functional solutions to create the most comfortable, inviting facility. Knowing what is on the market that functions for the elderly population will help interior designers sell their services.

Many seating companies provide firmer and higher cushions that make it easier for an elderly person to position in and out of a chair. Floor coverings that are easy to walk on, easy to look at, and easily cared for are also important. Colors that are desirable for the visually impaired person are necessary for nursing homes. Wayfinding is critical, especially when there are multiple wings or halls in a building.

Nursing homes have both indoor and outdoor spaces. Proper security is needed to monitor residents unable to leave the building alone. Making environments homelike yet protective and functional for residents, guests, and employees provides many challenges, all of which are opportunities for interior designers.

Interior designers are often the ones who help healthcare owners understand the critical environmental needs necessary for a successful business. Even though owners and employees spend many hours in a facility, it is important that the interior functions appropriately and is of suitable design for the residents who

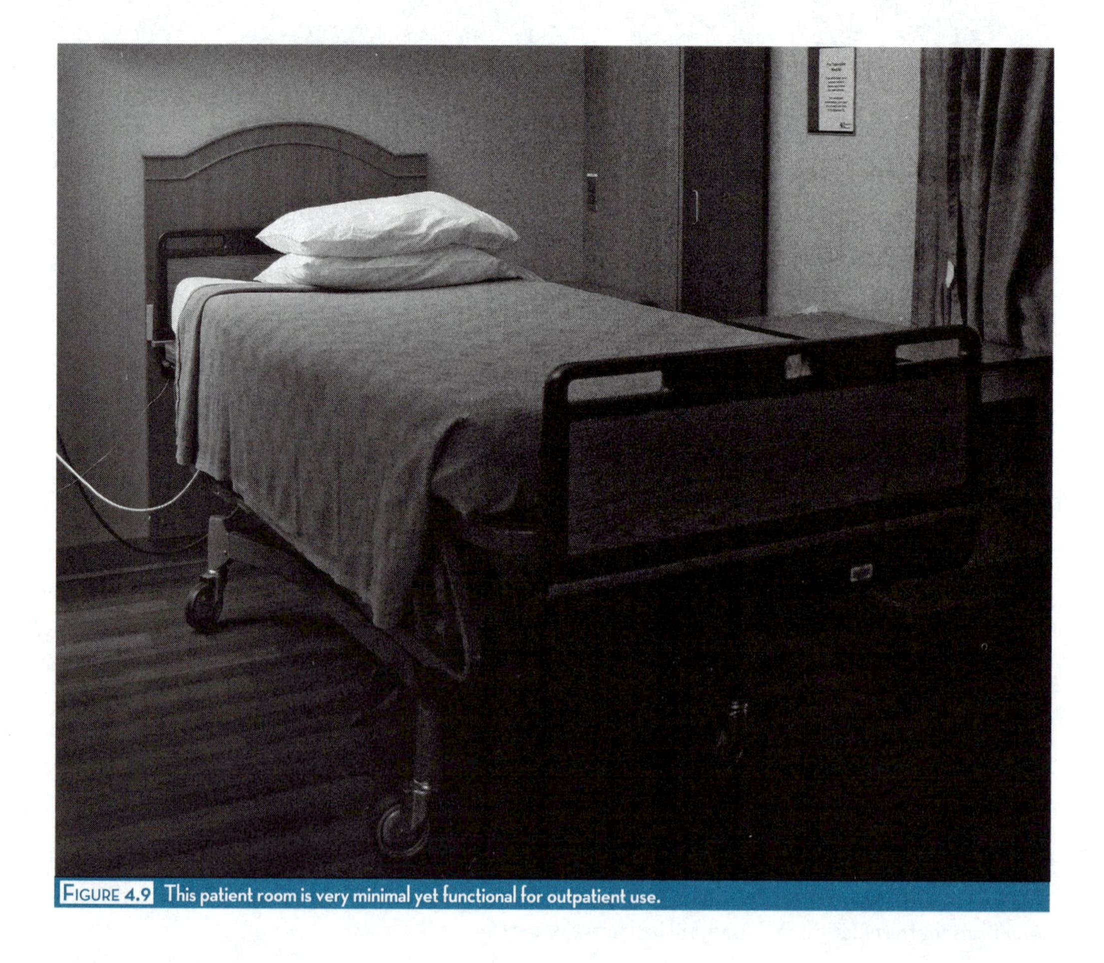

FIGURE 4.9 This patient room is very minimal yet functional for outpatient use.

must call these spaces home and whose money ensures a profitable business. It is sometimes necessary for professional interior designers to point out this priority to keep nurses, secretaries, or maintenance personnel from changing arrangements, colors, and furnishings they may be tired of.

Assisted Living

Assisted-living residences can range from a traditional home to a high-rise apartment building. Residences can be freestanding, housed within a nursing-home complex, or housed with other residential-living options. There are thousands of these residences and no specific blueprint for them.

The interior designer must comply with local building codes and fire-safety regulations as required for each location. An assisted-living situation encourages independence for each resident. An assisted-living residence is a combination of housing, personalized supportive services, and healthcare that is designed to meet individual needs. The healthcare is both scheduled and unscheduled.

Interior design for assisted living can be done for an assisted-care community or building. Interior design can also be for a private resident who is in an assisted-care location. Most interior design jobs for assisted living are done for the general environment. The private spaces are usually designed in such a way that residents can easily personalize their space with their own furnishings and accessories.

FIGURE 4.10 Additional furnishings, which usually belong to the resident, accent this extended-stay guest room.

Interior designers would approach an assisted-living project in much the same way as they would for an extended-care or nursing home design. All of these care environments have common areas for dining, access to health services, recreational areas for health promotion and exercise programs, housekeeping services, auxiliary offices, and chapel areas for religious services.

Health Clinics

Health clinics are privately owned or hospital-owned. Interior designers who work for large hospital corporations often do the interior design for clinics that are under the hospital's corporate umbrella. Sometimes, **standards** are designed for hospital-owned clinics. With this type of interior design, the interior designer might create three to five designs and then select one for each stand-alone facility. These would be updated every few years.

Some physicians choose to remain independent of a specific hospital. These health clinics usually have a more unique interior design. Independent healthcare providers often display their unique attitudes in their clinics' "look." These physicians typically spend more money on interior design.

Seating in health clinics is a numbers issue. The number of bodies that can wait for care is related to the amount of money that can be generated in a given day. An interior design challenge is to create a comfortable, well-spaced look using a maximum number of seats.

Sound is also an interior design challenge. Privacy is a requirement in all areas of healthcare. Clinics that were once very openly designed are now being divided into more spaces for privacy. Privacy policies can make the interior design and functions of health clinics less friendly and inviting because of these required closed spaces.

FIGURE 4.11 This glass partition allows some voice privacy while maintaining an open look.

FIGURE 4.12 These areas are separate, yet maintain an open look.

Physician Offices

As with health clinics, physician offices are either hospital-owned or privately owned. A similar philosophy with interior design services is apparent among physician offices. Patient privacy is once again an important aspect of the space planning. Doctors personalize and individualize their spaces and often have comfortable seating for themselves and patients. Doctors' offices are usually in a quiet location far from the reception area. Offices are accessorized and well-appointed. Physician offices can be part of a larger environment such as a hospital or health clinic, and the design theme compatible with the building as a whole.

A physician's office can be more personal in its interior design. Even though it is not always seen by patients, it is a personal space and can definitely be designed for the doctor instead of the patient. The interior design challenge is to create a unique office space that has continuity with the rest of the facility within which it is housed.

Unlike general healthcare spaces, physician offices are typically more elaborate in their interior design. Personal preferences dictate special artistic accessories, more elaborate wall coverings, window treatments, and furnishings, all of which can be design accents.

FIGURE 4.13 This private office is a restful space for the physician.

FIGURE 4.14 This private office interior displays personal items and interests of the physician.

Dental Offices

Privately owned dental offices are some of the most prosperous spaces for interior designers. The profession of dentistry is very aesthetic. Dental offices are becoming almost spa-like in their environment, with mood lighting, music, and comfortable and relaxing chairs. Dentistry is sometimes an optional service in healthcare.

Patients make regular visits to dental offices to get a routine checkup, have their teeth cleaned, have their teeth straightened, or receive any number of elective dental services. Patients also have dental emergencies, but most dental practices concern elective services.

Dental office interiors are very friendly, service-oriented spaces that still cater to the sometimes nervous and apprehensive patient. Cool color environments enhance most dental offices. Along with color, patients are exposed to many comfort items, relaxing areas, and people who guide them through a painless experience.

Services for patients include individual headsets for television or stereo, warmed blankets, and, in some offices, manicures. A host or hostess might help the patient navigate through their dental experience. Marketing high-end dentistry is a very big business and the interior environment plays a large role in the success of these healthcare offices. Dental offices also offer product sales for the convenience of the patient.

Within healthcare, dental offices are becoming a specialized profession for the interior designer. Some dental-office furnishings, equipment, and supply companies have **in-house interior designers**. This allows them to offer a total service for their dentist clients.

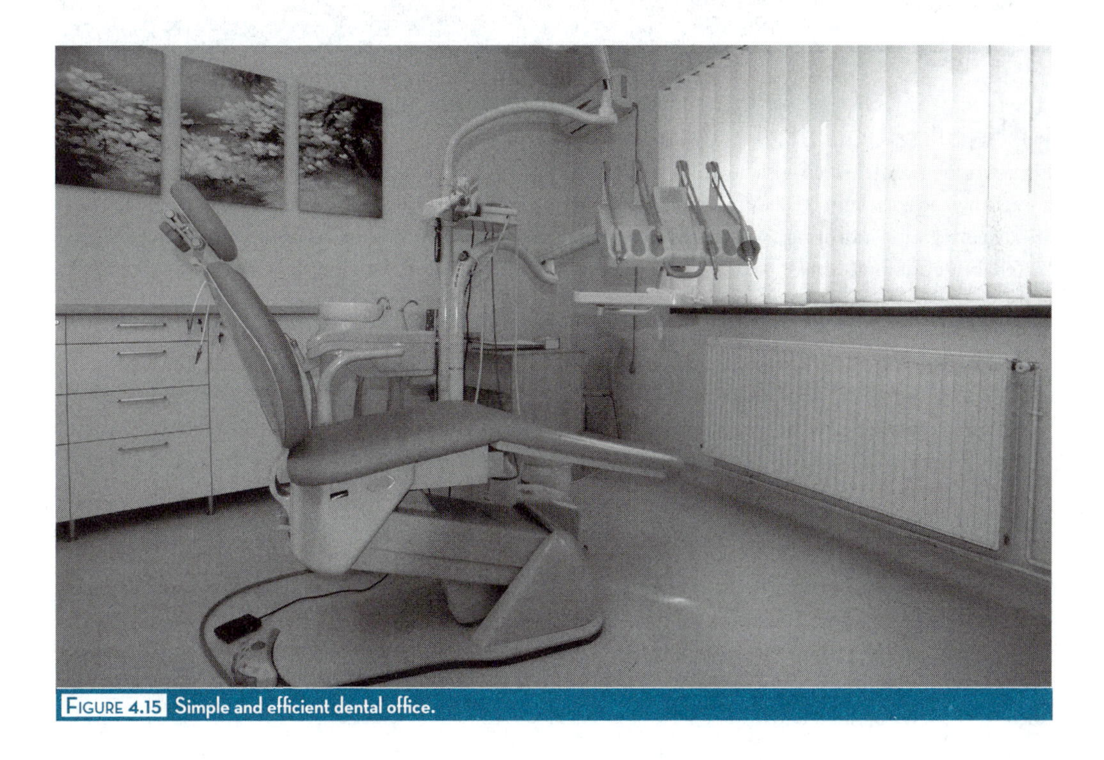

FIGURE 4.15 Simple and efficient dental office.

FIGURE 4.16 Well-displayed products are available in this dental office as the patients check out.

Rehabilitation and Fitness

Fitness is highly integrated with healthcare, especially as it relates to rehabilitation. Many of these facilities are also owned by hospitals. They include both separate facilities and places within a hospital campus. These are also integrated into other healthcare facilities such as nursing homes and assisted-living communities.

Rehabilitation and fitness within nursing homes and assisted-living situations are one way to integrate younger-aged people to create a more youthful environment. This brings energy to a primarily aging community.

Memberships are usually required for admittance to rehabilitation and fitness spaces. For healthcare employees, memberships are often part of the benefit package. Along with memberships comes competition for membership, and that requires marketing. Environments that compete for clientele are great for interior designers.

The interior design of a building is noticed before the services it offers are. The interior environment usually makes a difference in membership selection unless a doctor prescribes a hospital-owned facility. But even when a fitness center is hospital-owned, outside memberships are often sought. Outside memberships have separate costs relative to the person joining, where they work, and what healthcare system their insurance benefits cater to. Like doctor preferences, fitness facilities do not always match with insurance preferences.

The general public is sometimes willing to pay a premium for the facility of their choice. The selection of a rehabilitation and fitness center might be related to the center's other members or to a convenient location. The interior environment and the services offered will also influence selections.

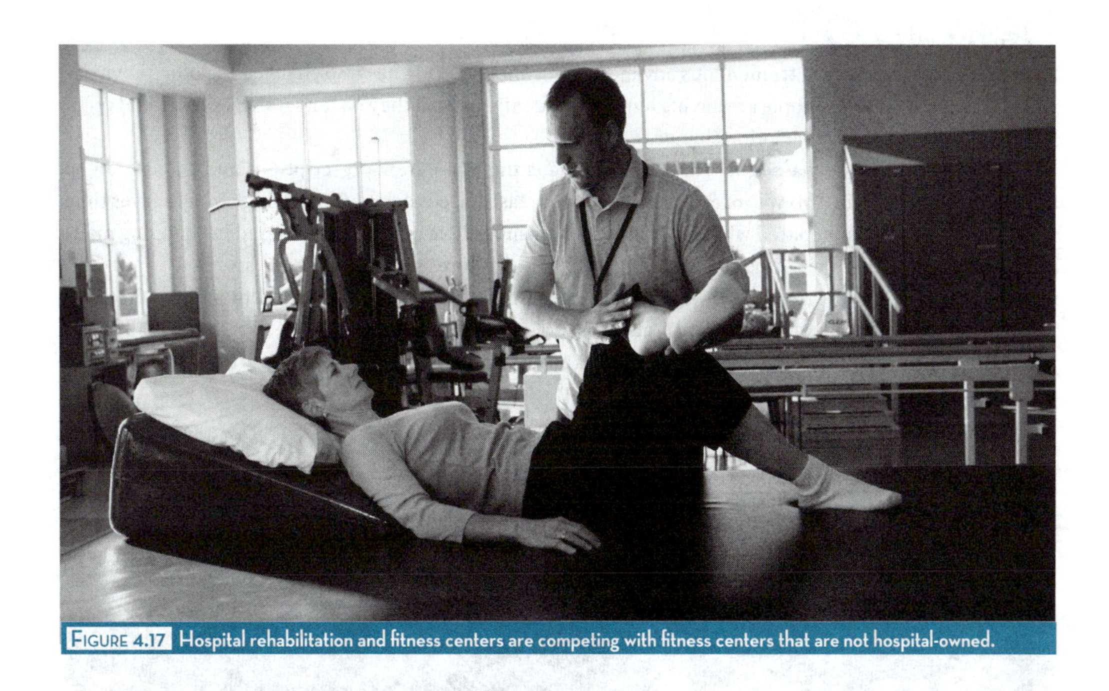

FIGURE 4.17 Hospital rehabilitation and fitness centers are competing with fitness centers that are not hospital-owned.

FIGURE 4.18 Snack areas and healthy-eating options are a plus for this rehab center.

Optometry Offices

Optometry has experienced tremendous advances in technology. This has also changed the office environment and function. More people are having lens implants, after which they no longer need glasses and regular optometry visits for prescription changes.

For those who require glasses, fast and fashionable is the issue. New prescriptions and frames can be available within an hour. This way of thinking fits into our fast-paced society. Combining services saves time and money. Eyewear is prepared while one eats lunch or shops. Eye care is often offered in shopping malls and hotels. An inviting environment to sell fashionable frames lures shoppers into the space.

Optional eye surgeries are a whole new area in healthcare marketing and services. Optometry offices are more like outpatient areas of general hospitals. Most are separate facilities. These services are usually elective, much like the dental business. Interior design is an important part of marketing for this expanding area in healthcare.

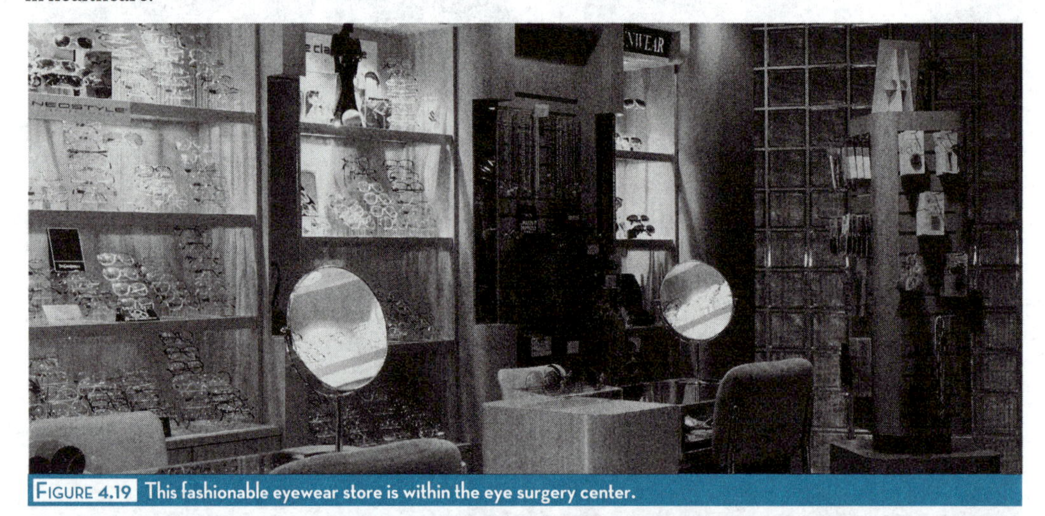

FIGURE 4.19 This fashionable eyewear store is within the eye surgery center.

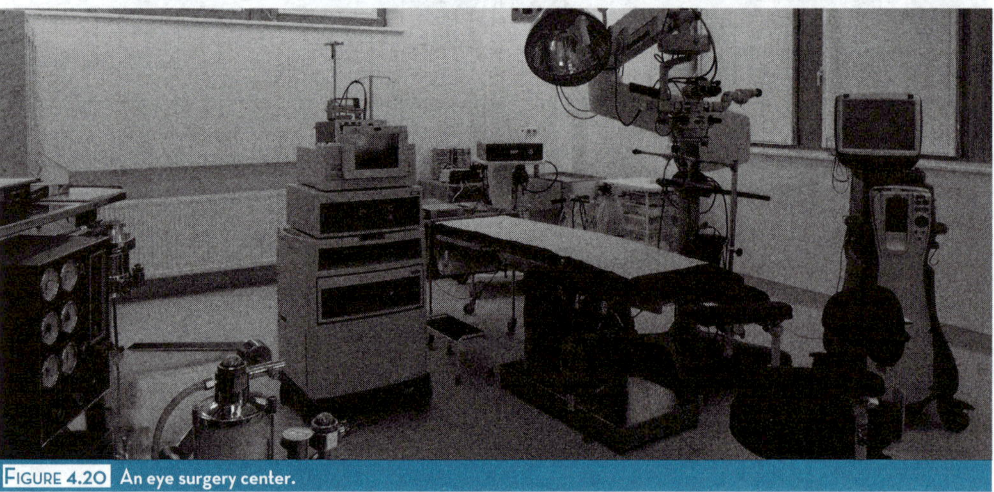

FIGURE 4.20 An eye surgery center.

Interior Designer Profile 4.1
Sherry Barton-Young, Owner, Creative Design Consultants, Inc., Springfield, Missouri

Sherry Barton-Young, an interior designer registered in Missouri, has a bachelor of fine arts with an emphasis in interior design from Drury University. She has specialized in healthcare design for more than 15 years. She began her career in commercial interior design working for a Herman Miller, Inc. office furniture dealership.

Barton-Young points out that healthcare is a very specialized area with many legal implications for practices and standards that include fire codes, infectious control, biohazards, and maintenance. There are rigorous guidelines that vary from state to state. No two jobs are alike.

Some healthcare companies are establishing "standards" for all their facilities; however, this takes the design ability out of the work. Having unique interiors is great.

According to Barton-Young, healthcare projects are cyclical. For example, she says, "they can be so 'vanilla' and then very colorful and then back to 'vanilla.' It is important to keep track of the market and the products that are current for this industry."

SUMMARY

The designer who wants an exacting, meaningful, and very relevant career in interior design should consider healthcare design. Research indicating that the health and well-being of patients increase with well-planned and aesthetically pleasing environments gives credibility to our concern over the design in a healthcare setting. This research continues to influence our choice of color, materials, lighting, the use of windows, and overall design. The designer's skills coupled with public demand have been instrumental in the improvements that we currently see in healthcare settings. We are no longer satisfied with a cold and sterile medicinal environment. We want relaxing, comfortable, safe, and functional places that meet our healthcare needs. Strong competition in the healthcare industry and public demand support design practitioners who want to invest their talent in this most rewarding career.

RELATED CAREER OPTIONS

Cabinet, Storage, and Closet Designer

Codes Specialist

Communications Specialist

Environmental Safety Specialist

Facilities Manager

Product Tester

Publicist

Purchasing Agent

Sourcing Specialist

Universal Designer

SKILLS AND APTITUDES An interior designer who wants to become involved in some aspect of healthcare design must have a genuine interest in medicine or health-related issues. Being detail-oriented and exacting when it comes to regulations and codes, and possessing extensive product knowledge relative to healthcare are all essential. The designer should be able to work with the healthcare staff, doctors, administrators, and most of all the general public, who, in this situation, is frequently not at its best.

The designer needs to see the patient as a whole person and design spaces accordingly. Understanding human psychology and health and wellness issues and having compassion and superior interpersonal skills would benefit the healthcare designer. It goes without saying that the designer needs to apply all the principles and elements of design to the facility at hand while realizing that the health, safety, and welfare of the patients is of primary concern. The beauty of the space will develop as the designer uses both creativity and care for the patient as the ultimate guide.

EDUCATION A bachelor degree in interior design from an accredited college or university is the preferred requirement but an associate degree is a good start. General education classes in psychology, health and human services, sociology, and fitness would be helpful. Electives such as gerontology, community and public health, facility management, and public relations are educational opportunities that would also be beneficial.

Most important, become board-certified with the American Academy of Healthcare Interior Designers (AAHID; www.aahid.org). See Chapter Nine, "Certified Specialty Areas," for details.

KEY TERMS

Environmental Psychology

In-House Designer

Standards

Universal Design

Wayfinding

DISCUSSION QUESTIONS

1. Discuss various internship possibilities that would prepare the interior design student for a career in healthcare.
2. How can the public areas of an assisted-living facility be designed so as to promote socializing and group interaction? How can the interior designer prepare for this challenge?
3. How can the aspiring designer determine whether or not the health-care field is going to be the right career choice?

CHAPTER FIVE
RETAIL

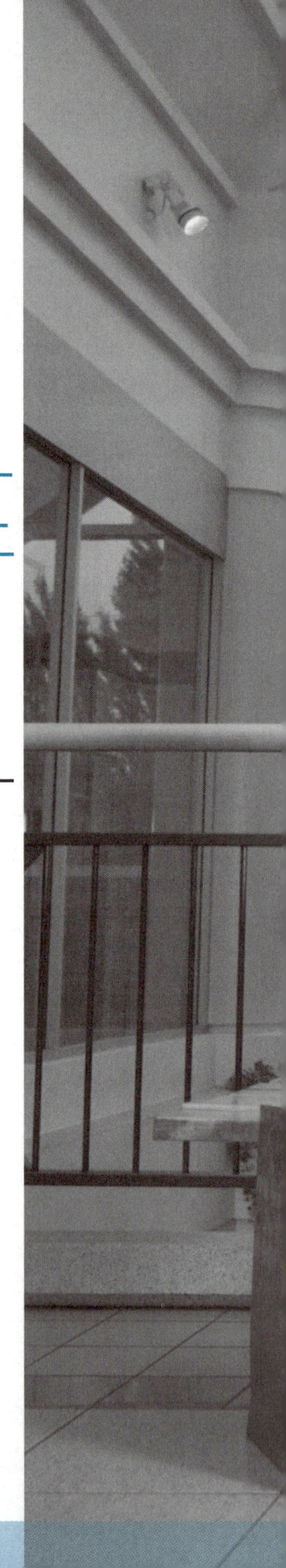

5

CHAPTER OBJECTIVES

After reading this chapter, you should be able to identify and understand areas in retail interior design, including: Store Planning • Window Display and Design • Mall Design • Chain Stores Boutiques • Big-Box Stores • Service Centers.

Retail design encompasses many different types of stores, selling every product imaginable. Selling and buying can be done in any number of ways, but how much fun is it to walk into a truly creative store with exciting displays, great color and light, and all things beautifully geared to put you in the mood to buy? Maybe it is a hardware store with pleasant surroundings, perfectly organized with efficient use of space, labeled well, and easy to navigate. The designer's role is comprehensive: Make the space look good, have plenty of display and storage, make the most of expensive retail space, and have the products look great. The retail space needs to be comfortable and safe, durable, and easy to maintain with high traffic. It should capture people's attention and induce them to stay and shop.

Store Planning

Retail-store planning is a specialty area in interior design, although huge in scope. There are design challenges that are unique to retail. There is the continual movement of products, which are not always the same size and shape. There can be a great deal of congestion at times and vacancy at others. Store lighting differs depending on where various products are located. Signage and labeling is important. Many times there are corporate guidelines that have to be met. Branding, **logos**, revolving merchandise, clearance sales, holiday rushes, and the constant pressure to sell merchandise also complicate the designer's job. Spaces are necessary for checkouts, window displays, dressing rooms, wrapping stations, customer service areas, and many other function areas involved in retail.

Interior designers sell themselves and their design ideas on all their projects; therefore, they are to some extent already experts at selling. With good and effective retail design, the interior designer is assisting the client in the area of selling. The store managers and salespeople know their products and the customers, but the designer can help present the products in a creative way so the customer can see the product in a new and enticing way. Space needs to be well-planned and designers need to know products and have many resources available to them to enhance environments, whatever the purpose.

Marketing is an important part of interior design for store planning. Knowing the market is the indicator that will help in planning for a particular segment of the population. For example, older citizens are growing in numbers and we can create spaces and provide products that are user-friendly, well-lit, easy to reach, and accessible for all. Know the merchandise and know the consumer.

An interior designer who is very creative and is willing to develop unique ideas in store planning will definitely be in demand in this career segment. The areas for consideration include: entrance, store size, store finishes, traffic patterns, merchandise planning, color planning, general lighting, display lighting, accent lighting, displays, props, furniture, and accessories.

FIGURE 5.1 This well-designed display encourages the customer to dream about how his or her own space could look.

FIGURE 5.2 This unique display attracts attention. (See color plate 9.)

Each store design involves specific space-planning considerations that will ensure the proper and complete function of the facility. Although a furniture store and a dress shop share a common goal—to sell merchandise—they obviously require different layouts to achieve that goal.

When designing a store, the interior designer needs to creatively present whatever merchandise is being sold in a way that enables the consumers to see themselves owning it, wearing it, or using it. Enhancing merchandise and making it appealing and desirable is very important.

What makes a person go into a store? What keeps them looking around and hopefully making a purchase? Often, the interior designer needs to create a *"wow"* factor to grab their attention. This can happen in many creative ways. An entrance that is very inviting is a good beginning.

Once inside a store, the clientele need to be able to move around comfortably and to locate items that they need or want with ease. A good design or presentation is often the reason that an item is purchased. This has little to do with need.

Retail interior designers can be extremely good at merchandising and at presentation of merchandise. Eye-catching displays that are unique and different will grab the consumer's attention.

Store planning requires that the interior designer knows what is on the market for store fixtures and furnishings. Store planning is an industry that has a unique set of furniture for the purpose of display. Many interior designers also take advantage of antique furnishings for creative displays. The creative thinker sees few boundaries in using recycled items.

Window Display and Design

"A picture is worth a thousand words." A window display is a picture that silently sells something. Window displays can create a dramatic effect with the use of color and light. Drama is the effect to strive for in window displays. For example, a window with all items in white could be highlighted with colored lighting. This display could constantly change by varying the color of light. Another unique display idea is to use an object that is out of context. This technique is very common in advertising. An example is an advertisement for a faucet that shows a model wearing a dress that has a pattern of the advertised faucet design.

Professional organizations and specific industries, such as the window treatment industry, have yearly competitions where interior designers create fashion using the products from the company they are coupled with. The result of these competitions is a fabulous fashion show. These fashion shows are typically great fund-raisers.

There are many very fun display ideas using the out-of-character design concept. Another example is having a china or pottery display where the dishes are presented to look like dancers. This window display would cause one to look more than once; it would have an element of entertainment.

Repetition of products can also be very dramatic. This can be a specific style of dress or an entire collection of outerwear that is in the same printed fabric. The same concept can be used with several sofas or car styles that are presented in the same pattern or color.

A display that is well-designed shows many elements of good design. Scale and proportions are very important. Sometimes unique and out-of-character scale can create a dramatic look. This could be done with either larger-than-life or smaller-than-life scale.

FIGURE 5.3 Using unlikely materials for a fashion statement makes for great eye-catching advertising.

FIGURE 5.4 This out-of-character grass is an interesting paint look. (See color plate 10.)

FIGURE 5.5 This architecture is an example of both out-of-character and dramatic design elements.

FIGURE 5.6 Repetition is a valuable design tool.

FIGURE 5.7 This monochromatic display is very dramatic. (See color plate 11.)

FIGURE 5.8 Out-of-scale items can be a fun way to attract attention.

Window design and display is definitely for the creative interior designer who thinks outside the normal parameters. Interior designers who find inspiration from many and all elements in the world are great in this industry. These designers collect ideas everywhere they go and from all that they do—a visit to a museum, a walk in the park, or a book or magazine article.

Window design and display is an area that is constantly being critiqued. The critiques are both conscious and unconscious. If a person walked down a major shopping area street or mall, there would only be a select group of windows or perhaps only one that would fall into the "wow" category. Regardless of the interior design area of interest, the best work always stands out and those designers are the sought-after professionals.

Mall Design

Mall design encompasses an overall space that includes many individual stores. Malls typically house both specialty shops and chain stores, and each store has a look that is separate from the overall look of the mall. With numerous stores and a variety of layouts, directional signage, within both shops and public areas, is an important part of mall design.

Malls are sometimes located within another type of building. They might be in or connected to an office complex, hotel, convention center, or casino.

Each mall has its own specific, unique design. The shape of the mall footprint helps dictate the overall look. The style of the mall—sprawling, condensed, open-air, floor number—all dictate style. Products can help define the design and the design can help sell products.

Primary elements to consider when designing a mall include: the size of the mall; the number of parking spaces; the proximity of parking to the mall; and the signage, both exteriors to be seen from the highway or street, and interiors within the parking areas and upon entering the mall. Mall location is also a design factor because each region or country has both material and climate considerations. Some malls are enclosed while others are open-air.

CAREER TIP

Window displays can make all the difference in a passerby's decision to stop and shop.

FIGURE 5.9 The design of this mall has much to say about its location.

Malls accommodate the consumer as well as the delivery truck. These usually require separate entrances. The truck traffic needs to be relatively separate from the general mall traffic. Deliveries need to happen without disturbing the sales area.

Like other commercial interior design, more than one wayfinding method is required for malls. Large department stores have numerous entrances and exits that can be very confusing when trying to locate your parked automobile.

The space between and outside the shops is an important design consideration. This space can resemble a park or street, or incorporate lounge environments, play areas, or entertainment venues. Creative thinking in the use and feel of the public space is another interior design opportunity.

Malls also need to accommodate basic services such as restrooms, first aid, and areas for occasional seating. Function, safety, comfort, and convenience are important for mall design just as they are for other spaces an interior designer plans.

Chain Stores

Chain store interiors are duplicated for a consistent look regardless of location. Identification usually begins with the signage and floor plan layout. Merchandise sometimes changes per region.

Regardless of the chain store location, items within the store are similarly located and readily found by the

FIGURE 5.10 Public spaces for relaxing within a mall are a welcome addition.

familiar shopper. This is true with numerous types of chain stores, such as grocery stores and name-brand department stores.

Because of the number of items required for multiple stores, chain store owners can take advantage of volume pricing for interior products. Custom wall coverings with store logos can be incorporated with very little extra cost, creating a very impressive image.

Many chain store companies have **in-house** interior designers and warehouses that contain store fixtures, furnishings, and accessories to accommodate interior design additions, merchandise changes, and redesigns for numerous locations.

CAREER TIP

Stores should be easy to navigate. Traffic patterns are very important in planning retail space.

Keeping the latest, updated interior design is important in retail merchandising. Unless the chain store is in the used and recycled business, consumers expect to see the latest styles and colors, including in the store's own interior design.

Chain stores are like all consumer-driven businesses. The interior designer needs to create a design that is unique and one that makes a difference. This helps to create more traffic. Lots of traffic usually translates into more business and more profit.

Sometimes the difference is an in-house coffee shop, restaurant, or elaborate restroom or lounge. Chain stores constantly work on ways to get more customers inside their store. User-friendly services are definitely one of the current trends.

Even automobile dealership showrooms offer their customers an extreme amount of comfort. Everything from cookies, fresh fruit, beverages, movies, and electronic services are available, especially in the upscale dealerships.

When considering the interior design for chain stores, new ideas that will create more store interest are definitely a sales tool.

Interior designers also need to understand the details of lighting for merchandising. When consumers shop, they typically need to be able to clearly see the product they are interested in purchasing. If exact color is important, full-spectrum lightbulbs are necessary. Incorporating natural light is also great when possible.

Boutiques

Boutiques showcase specialty products. This is commonly and most successfully done in a more unique and different way than in other retail establishments. Creative uses for both new and old products and spaces are important for great boutique interiors.

Boutiques also have a very specific clientele and offer sales-related functions catering to them. A small specialty

CAREER TIP

Featured items on display or advertised for sale need to be locatable within the store.

store might host a fund-raiser for a needy cause, a wine-and-cheese party to promote a new line, a trunk show, or a special sale for a select group of clients. The designer may be instrumental in providing special accessories or display items to do this. The furnishings for a retail shop need to be flexible and support the products and space. Boutique shoppers are usually looking for individual attention, customer service, and items that are not found in the **big-box stores.**

Maintaining a successful boutique is about customer relationships. Special services include numerous details such as gift wrapping, beverage and snack service while shopping, **trunk shows** showcasing new products, guest artists, and special topic speakers. Interior designers are sometimes asked to work on logo designs and special promotional materials.

Boutiques are located in many places. Typically they are near or in other shopping spaces. Boutiques can be as unique in their locations as they are in their general character. They can also be totally separate from other shopping areas because the clientele often seeks them out, either for their location, their price range, or their inventory of specialty items. Boutiques do not necessarily appeal to the general public; if they are unique or specific enough in nature, they do not depend on traffic from adjacent shops. They might benefit from an exclusionary location, or one less expensive due to the selective category of their products.

Boutique interior design offers great custom-design opportunities in retail. Boutique owners definitely look for the most unique presentations for their store. Boutiques usually showcase more **one-of-a-kind** items. This type of store might sell original artwork, original furniture designs, handcrafted items such as blown glass, fiber art, or reclaimed items that have been given new life.

FIGURE 5.11 These displays show the uniqueness of this upscale boutique.

Logo boutiques can incorporate their unique logo into floor designs, fabric patterns, stairway cutouts, or furnishings designed to look like the logo. Some logos work better for this than others. Repetition of the boutique logo is desirable where possible.

A boutique interior design usually changes with color and fashion trends. When redesigning boutique interiors, all surfaces including the ceiling need to be considered. Keeping current on future color forecasting is another important tool that applies to all the interior design careers.

Big-Box Stores

Big-box stores are warehouse-type structures where high volume is emphasized over high profit margins. The big-box stores are usually very large, though size does vary with the kind of products that are being sold. A big-box eyeglass store would take up much less space than a big-box furniture store.

Because the buildings are warehouse styles, the interior image is also warehouse-like. Some are designed to have a more finished look while others emphasize the unfinished look of a warehouse. These buildings are large, open spaces that are on one level.

Big-box stores are stand-alone or grouped in a big-box-store marketing area where several similar stores share very large parking lots. The big-box store concept is based on volume, speed, and convenience.

Service is seldom part of the big-box store. Even large furniture items do not include installation or delivery. This varies with each big-box store. Consumers usually take this into consideration when purchasing large items or merchandise that might require servicing.

Big-box stores are frequently chain stores that have in-house interior designers and planners. One interior design concept is duplicated as many times as there are locations. As merchandise changes, the interior designs of these warehouses are adjusted.

FIGURE 5.12 Big-box stores are getting more creative with their warehouse facilities.

Interior design for big-box stores is about displaying large amounts of inventory. Creating new ways to stack merchandise and finding new display ideas for massive amounts of product is the interior design challenge with these stores.

Lighting design is important because there is very little if any natural light in a warehouse. Multiple types of fixtures and multiple height placements can add interest to these basic large-box spaces.

Keeping the traffic patterns within these stores moving comfortably, without the consumer feeling crowded, is helpful. Signage is a large part of the interior design in a big-box store. When so many displays have a similar look, location information is a must. Signage is usually hung from the ceiling.

Displaying volumes of products and having the merchandise accessible and within reach can be challenging. The merchandise stock is usually housed on shelving above or behind each item. Depending on the big-box store design, merchandise is also stored inside various merchandise display units.

Interior designers who specialize in the design of big-box stores constantly work on display and function. Store layout is a big part of the interior planning. In keeping with the warehouse/low-budget appearance, materials on the floors, walls, and ceilings are very minimal.

As the kinds of superstores increase, selling different types of inventory, their interior spaces will become a more competitive environment. The basic, unadulterated warehouse environment—concrete floors, metal shelving—may need to be improved upon to maintain interest and attract customers. This competition will require more thought in the interior design of these very basic warehouse spaces.

Service Centers

There are many types of storefronts—shops providing services of various kinds. Hair and nail salons, tanning and various grooming and spa salons, massage therapy centers, and other personal treatment and beauty shops need to attract customers. There are repair shops, alteration services and cleaners, mailing and post offices, hobby shops, and car washes. The design of all these buildings needs to reflect the services offered. They should appear clean, organized, and efficient.

Food centers need to be especially enticing. Advertising, name recognition, reputation, and food discounts bring attention to the markets, but clean, durable, well-lit, and attractive decor makes the food look more appetizing. Research has shown that certain colors stimulate appetite and we know that when you feel hungry, you purchase more.

Food centers would include bakeries and candy shops, butcher shops, gourmet markets, and ethnic food stores. Eye appeal is certainly a lure, both in the foods presented and how the foods are presented and that is where the designer comes in. Food service meets basic needs and takes many expanded forms: catering, raw foods, and partially prepared meals that the customer finishes at home. Entire kitchens and equipment are available for public use; consumers select a menu, go by after work and assemble the meal, then take it home and reheat, saving shopping time, energy, and cleanup. Again, these types of businesses need to be clean, safe, and facilitate quick preparation, plus be comfortable and visually attractive.

Regardless of the type of retail establishment, good business practices, great eye appeal, and functionality are necessary to ensure a profitable venture, and designers, with skill and talent, can help make that happen.

Interior Designer Profile 5.1: Carla Drysdale, Owner, Nancy Rose Inc., Springfield, Missouri

Specializing in fine linens, sleepwear, bath and spa, and interior design, Carla Drysdale earned her bachelor of science in interior design from Missouri State University. Her store is unique. Not every customer who walks into the store plans to become a client; however, some evolve after finding out about the design resources available. The store attracts both walk-in customers and clients looking for a professional interior designer.

The retail displays in Drysdale's store emphasize interior design. In her store, displays are changed every six weeks. The window displays change every two months. The store keeps a lot of custom products available and combines them with standard items to satisfy a range of clientele. High-end linens also have yardage available for custom products. Nancy Rose uses several independent workrooms for custom design.

The small boutique only stocks basic linens and a representation of fabrics from custom companies that are also available. This is not typical of other interior design retail stores. Many boutiques carry a variety of products, while Nancy Rose is very specialized in in-stock merchandise. What the customers soon find out is that Nancy Rose is a comprehensive resource for all design needs and offers professional assistance.

Drysdale is inspired by the many interior design markets she attends—approximately six each year. She emphasizes newly available products and very current and up-to-date design styles. Style options include the very sophisticated, traditional, contemporary, classic, and any other style preferred by the client.

Drysdale's recommendations for designers interested in retail are: be prepared to work long hours, be a multitasker, be a jack-of-all-trades, know as much as possible about accounting and business, have great communication skills, be willing to manage employees, know as much as possible about sales, and believe in what you are doing.

SUMMARY

Interior designers working in retail interior design are inspired by the challenge of constantly changing displays and merchandise and by the continuous opportunity to exhibit creative work. The career options in retail are as varied as the types of stores.

RELATED CAREER OPTIONS

- Acoustic Designer
- ADA Specialist
- Advertising Professional
- Architectural Space Planner
- Colorist
- Commercial Floor and Carpet Designer
- Commercial and Industrial Designer
- Construction Firm Professional
- Contract Designer
- Cost Estimator
- Design Contractor
- Development Model Designer
- Exhibit Designer
- Furniture Retail Salesperson
- Hospitality Designer
- In-House Corporate Designer
- Journalist
- Lighting Analyst
- Mall Designer
- Manufacturer's Representative
- Market Researcher
- Merchandise Display Designer
- Package Designer
- Photographer
- Property Manager
- Publicist
- Restaurant Designer
- Retail Designer
- Sales Representative
- Showroom Designer
- Space Planner
- Stairway Designer
- Trend Forecaster
- Universal Designer
- Visual Merchandiser
- Window Designer

SKILLS AND APTITUDES Skills and aptitudes in business, marketing, sales, and merchandising are helpful for a design career focusing on retail. Knowledge of and experience in those areas inform the designer about the particular needs and functions of retail spaces. Being able to understand and "read" the public is important. Needs change, as do lifestyles, and the designer should be sensitive to these changes. Design is not static and the retailer needs to be able to anticipate what the public will want. Changes in society, lifestyles, technology, materials, and demographics demand that the retailer pay attention, observe, and listen.

EDUCATION A bachelor degree in interior design combined with a minor in business, marketing, merchandising, or any other related field provides a great foundation. An associate degree also provides the educational background to get started. Some retail professionals also move up the ladder based on great design skill, refined after years of experience and innate talent. As much as education is valued in our society, we cannot fail to appreciate those who work hard and are dedicated to their craft. Innate ability is a true gift.

KEY TERMS

- Big-Box Store
- In-House
- Logo
- One of a Kind
- Trunk Show

DISCUSSION QUESTIONS

1. Discuss how the interior design of a retail store can affect sales of the products in the store.
2. Discuss why a designer should be familiar with business and marketing when designing for a retail store.

CHAPTER SIX

HOTELS, RESTAURANTS, AND HOSPITALITY

Fresh
Drinks

CHAPTER OBJECTIVES

After reading this chapter, you should be able to identify and understand the interior design needs for hospitality and restaurant facilities such as: Hotels • Motels • Restaurants • Fast-Food Establishments • Coffee Shops • Convention Centers • Casinos • Clubs.

The business of hotel, restaurant, and hospitality design can be very exciting and gratifying. People seek these environments for relaxation, entertainment, vacation, or simply to have a quiet meal at the end of a long day. The design of these interiors sets the tone and the emotion, and can dramatically affect the level of enjoyment. The settings can contribute a great deal to the contentment of the patrons and ultimately to the success of the establishment. Knowing that your design efforts can make such a difference in people's experience can be extremely rewarding. This area of commercial design can be financially worthwhile as well.

Hotels and Motels

Facilities of accommodation can be divided into two categories: hotels, establishments that provide lodging and often dining, entertainment, and personal services; and motels, lodging that typically provide limited services and where the rooms are usually accessible from the parking lot.

HOTELS

Global and regional travel have brought about new looks in the hotel industry. Hotels have become more than just a place to sleep between travel destinations. They are frequently the destination itself, as well as a place to sleep. Convenience is one of the main keys to marketing today's hotels. Uniqueness is another important factor for interior designers to capitalize on. Travelers impressed by their hotel's design and accommodations provide great advertising; they typically enjoy discussing their travel experiences.

FIGURE 6.1 The Sanderson Hotel in London has fabulous design elements everywhere you look. (Steve Curtis of Space Design Studios, www.bardesign.co.uk.)

Interior designers have many opportunities for creative thinking, and hotels are perfect for this. **Adaptive reuse** is often a creative way to utilize interesting buildings, some with character, some iconic, some simply discarded and deteriorating. Adapting some structures for reuse is in alignment with sustainable practices. Thinking of new rooms and uses for unused spaces such as old train cars, 18-wheeler trailers, old schoolhouses, vacant warehouses, or caves is not only environmentally responsible but provides unique and creative design solutions. New ideas for old items and spaces are the wave of our sustainable future.

FIGURE 6.2 This creative use of space in the train car rooms at the Crowne Plaza Hotel and Conference Center at Historic Union Station in Indianapolis offers a fun and unique hotel experience.

Individual spaces such as the train-car room in Figure 6.2 are also great add-ons to existing buildings. Adding space without new construction saves time as well as money. An example of this is an English hotel made of modified steel shipping containers. The 120-room hotel took about four months to construct on-site.

This idea was generated by Verbus Systems, a UK contractor. The steel shipping containers were fitted with hotel fixtures in Shenzhen, China, and then transported to England by boat. This modular concept is great for additions as well as for quickly responding to growing markets.

FIGURE 6.3 This grand hotel makes the guest feel like royalty.

FIGURE 6.4A & 6.4B The Beckham Creek Cave Haven in Arkansas offers an experience that is difficult to describe—a must-visit place.

Unusual space can be very thought-provoking. Interior designers, like other artists, enjoy a canvas on which to be creative. Having a unique space conjures up new thoughts and ideas. Travelers enjoy different experiences and hotels can offer memorable ones.

CAREER TIP

Dramatic contrasts create vivid first impressions.

Because hotels are part of the destination, amenities within the hotels are an important feature. Some of the many extras offered by hotels are: office, living, and dining areas in addition to the bedroom space; Internet service; in-room video entertainment; refrigerators and microwaves; snacks; spa-like bathrooms; fitness equipment areas; indoor pools; laundry facilities; dry cleaning; childcare facilities; restaurants; nightclubs; meeting and convention rooms; shops; assistance locating all area attractions; and a host of other services.

In selecting the interior design of a hotel, the professional needs to consider first the geographical area, then the kind of look and type of materials that would be appropriate for the hotel location.

While traveling in Pierre, South Dakota, one hotel had a sign on top of an old-looking washcloth in the bathroom that read: "Please use for makeup removal and cleaning guns." It was amusing, but also appropriate for the area that is home to the Varmint Hunters Association. A rustic look for the interior was certainly appropriate for this very quaint capital city hotel.

Regardless of the area in the world, the hotel that is enhanced by and capitalizes on its location is especially pleasant. Hotels that appear to grow out of the side of a mountain and look like they were carefully and purposefully planned are usually well-appointed on the interior as well. Many of these well-planned structures begin with the interior design and evolve to include the outside. The outside of the building often dictates the inside appointments but the inside embellishments can inspire the outside as well. Ideally, there is compatibility between the two. Depending on the climate and the season, the inside often overflows to the outdoors and becomes an extension of that living space. A scenic view and big windows draw the eyes outward. Colors and materials from nature can also tie the inside and outside together, which is particularly impressive in a vacation setting.

The Hotel del Coronado hotel and spa in California offers great historic walking tours for both guests and visitors. This fabulous wooden structure located on the beach was the backdrop for the movie *Some Like It Hot,* starring Marilyn Monroe, Tony Curtis, and Jack Lemmon. This national historic landmark has been host to numerous politicians and celebrities, and even has its own famous ghost! The interior design of this great hotel and its tantalizing history create a memorable experience for all who stay here. It is often the history of a place that inspires both great design and a building's **historic preservation**—especially a building whose walls have housed and witnessed intriguing lives. The place, its history, and the people who enjoy it give added meaning to the designer's role.

Hotels provide a living space for numerous types of travelers with many different needs. Some travelers want to sleep late while others like to get up early. There are multiple noise levels and a need for many types of lighting and light control.

Hotel sizes vary a great deal. Smaller hotels, sometimes called inns, can be extremely quaint and very personal. Travelers who enjoy small hotels with special character often return to the same location for the comfortable and familiar feeling. These hotels are often difficult to get a room in because the clientele book rooms at least a year in advance.

FIGURE 6.5A & 6.5B The Hilton Promenade at Branson Landing, Missouri, is a center for shopping, dining, and live Branson-style entertainment.

FIGURE 6.6A & 6.6B The rooms of the Loews Ventana Canyon Resort hotel in Arizona offer the same angles and character as the structure, which fits snugly into the mountain landscape.

The interior designs of the most popular hotels have something special to offer. It might be a homey environment, an extremely elegant environment, or a very rustic, yet romantic, environment. Interior designers are challenged to express a look and feel that meets the needs of a specific area and of a sought-after clientele.

Some famous historic hotel **renovations** are taking on a modern, out-of-character look. Instead of the old traditional flavor of design, using heavy textiles and dark wood furnishings, they have taken on a very chic and ostentatious look. Some of the new contemporary looks have included wine-, cheese-, and chocolate-tasting rooms. The concept of contemporary elegance also includes sustainable, or "green," products. Where possible, hotels offer enhanced views of nature.

Interior designers who take every opportunity to design can be very successful in creating these public living spaces. Hotel spaces are increasingly very expensive. It is common to have hotel suites with multiple bedrooms and bathrooms that cost thousands of dollars per night.

When designing the interior for hotels, design professionals need to keep the health, safety, and welfare of the general public in mind, regardless of the interior design budget. All furnishings, fabrics, and finishes need to comply with **state codes** and regulations. Durability and maintenance are very important selection criteria.

Interior designers need to consider the need to replace furnishings and finishes in independent areas or individual rooms without compromising the interior design of the hotel. Continuity in hotel design has the same level of importance as with any well-planned interior.

MOTELS

Motels are designed to accommodate the traveler who wants to park right outside the door. Even though many motels are multistory structures, the doors usually open directly to the exterior of the building.

Motels usually have food choices that are separate businesses, adjacent to the motel. Accommodations are usually simple, with fewer extras than would be found at a hotel. Travelers who need little more than a place to sleep typically select motels.

Interior designers have different considerations when designing for motels. Walking directly into the room from the parking lot dictates that weather conditions should partly determine the types of finishes that would be most durable and safe. The direction the room faces, the window sizes, and the window treatments would dictate some of the necessary lighting needs.

Both hotels and motels need adequate **ambient lighting** and task lighting for the entire space. Interior designers need to work very closely with the electrical contractor so that all necessary lighting, outlets, and switches function properly and conveniently to accommodate guests.

Room furnishings and accessories in motels are often attached to the walls, the ceiling, or connected to other pieces of furniture. This helps prevent losses. Interior designers need to be aware of what is available for locking down furnishings and accessories. Creativity can also play a major role in minimizing the furnishings without creating a sparse-looking guest room. These security details should not be obvious to a guest.

Window treatments in these away-from-home places usually allow for the space to be totally dark any time of day or night. This can be accomplished with a separate window treatment or drapery lining. The way that window treatments open and close also needs to be obvious to the guest in order to ensure adequate longevity for the products.

FIGURE 6.7A & 6.7B The elaborate Hotel del Coronado is a favorite destination with its beach backdrop and its historic background.

COLOR**PLATE**1

The color contrasts in this space create a very pleasant visual.

COLOR**PLATE**2

The light colors in this room help give it a more spacious feeling.

COLOR**PLATE**3

The historical color collection in this dining room emphasizes the period design.

COLOR**PLATE**4

This color scheme offers a dramatic contrast of color.

COLOR**PLATE**5

A soft and quiet color scheme is conducive for study in this school library.

COLOR**PLATE**6

A contrasting headwall draws the student's attention to the front of the room.

COLOR**PLATE**7

Dramatic jewel tones are perfect for this school auditorium.

COLOR**PLATE**8

Color can offer additional help with wayfinding.

COLOR**PLATE**9

This unique display attracts attention.

COLOR**PLATE**10

This out-of-character grass is an interesting paint look.

COLORPLATE 11

This monochromatic display is very dramatic.

COLOR**PLATE**12

The interior design of this Maxim's restaurant in Hong Kong is colorful, crisp, contemporary, and inviting.

COLOR**PLATE**13

The luxury of a cruise is definitely reflected in the interior design of the ship.

Restaurants

Restaurants come in every shape, size, and style, along with every location and available cuisine. Regardless of the size of a city, most have restaurants as additions to hotel and motel accommodations. Restaurant choices are also similar, regardless of the city population, but there are many novelty places that attract diners based on the experience in addition to the food. There is a restaurant in southwest Missouri called Lambert's Cafe, The Only Home of Throwed Rolls, where the dinner rolls are actually thrown to the hungrily drooling diners from across the room (you better be a good catch). Of course, for this to work, open space planning and a very informal and rustic atmosphere must contribute to the theme. Other dining experiences—from dinner theaters to entertainment and food on a paddle-wheel boat, from dining in a cave to eating in a tree house—bridge the gap between entertainment and eating. For many of us, eating is entertainment and a creative designer helps solidify this connection. There is no limit to the imaginative and inventive establishments that enrich our lives and our stomachs.

Twenty-four-hour options for restaurants are available in major metropolitan areas. Hotels usually offer restaurant choices that consider dining time, price, and formality. Restaurants also position themselves near motels and hotels to accommodate travelers.

When designing restaurants, the psychology of color is important. People eat more food when dining in an environment that has a warm color scheme. The saliva glands work better with reds, oranges, and yellows. It is profitable for the restaurant to have customers with active saliva glands.

FIGURE 6.8 This restaurant's seating offers a variety of dining options, comfort, and privacy.

The type of seating and placement of the furnishings is important in a restaurant. Many people do not enjoy sitting in close proximity to a stranger in a restaurant. Most everyone has experienced the long booth with many small tables and a chair or two on the opposite side. This is typically done to accommodate more people. This is the kind of restaurant layout where return clientele (or the lack thereof) could make a significant difference. Many people who go out for quiet conversation feel uncomfortable in close proximity to strangers without any implied or actual barriers. For others, the opportunity to meet new people is part of the fun; for these diners, close contact is a positive thing. Designers need to assess the intended clientele, or

FIGURE 6.9 The very creative use of design is worth a trip to this restaurant.

vary the seating arrangements, in order to attract and comfort the various patrons.

Even the best food can seldom support restaurants with $17 chairs. An absolute "dive" that is successful usually has some very unique characteristics that include the interior design or lack thereof.

An elegantly designed and appointed restaurant with great food requires appropriate table coverings. Tablecloths made of fabric are most formal; however, some upscale restaurants also use paper tablecloths.

CAREER TIP

When designing restaurant lighting, highlight food, faces, art, and traffic patterns.

Seating is a very important component in all restaurants. The public comes in many sizes and seating is not "one size fits all." In order to facilitate all customer sizes, a variety of seating types are selected for most restaurants. The placement and interior design of more than one or two seating options varies depending on each restaurant and probably each interior designer.

Knowing what is on the market is an important job of the interior design professional. Depending on the project, custom designs are also important. Knowing the market keeps interior designers from reinventing what is already available. One example of a custom dining area might be that every chair around a large dining table looks like a different type of vegetable.

Restaurant lighting is an interior design opportunity. Enhancing the food and the clientele without totally highlighting the entire space is desired. The clientele also need to be able to see those they are dining with as opposed to a light fixture.

Acoustics in a restaurant help create a desired ambiance. An Italian restaurant where the waiters sing would have different finishes than an Italian restaurant that was very formal and intimate. Regardless of the cuisine, the interior design needs to function for the desired and specific clientele.

Interior designers can definitely make a difference. An example of this is the numerous privately owned chain restaurants that have been uniquely designed by the owner's choice of interior design professional as opposed to a chain restaurant that has its own corporate interior designer. A franchise with distinctive decor is the Cheesecake Factory. All of its installations are replicas of each other. It is the name, reputation, and style recognition (in addition to the food) that keeps the seats full. Hard Rock Cafe is another example of franchise similarity. People have a meal while they enjoy looking at all the entertainment memorabilia, including clothing, pictures, and awards—all geared to attract interested fans. Many times, the design of a restaurant, especially privately owned, has a theme of some sort; these include sports, artists, entertainers, an event that took place on the premises or elsewhere, and icons of all types that inspire the decor.

Many times, corporations insist on the same look to help with name-recognition. Sometimes there is enough name-recognition because of a well-established logo that the interior design can take on a unique look for each different location.

CAREER TIP

Designing with appropriate acoustical features can enhance public experiences in otherwise loud spaces.

FAST FOOD

Many fast-food restaurants have a trademarked look. These looks are created by the floor plan, color schemes, lighting, wall coverings, and seating or lack of seating. Fast-food restaurants do not always include dining areas.

One of the most important interior design issues is how comfortable and pleasing the space is for its clientele. Interior design needs to facilitate the functions of the space in order to be successful.

Fast-food restaurants can be upscale or ordinary in their interior design. Some are redesigning their image to be more contemporary or **retro**. The Maxim's Group fast-food restaurants in Hong Kong are an example of this. These fast-food restaurants look extremely artistic, colorful, clean, and inviting. An ordinary fast-food restaurant might have that "hometown" feel, a comforting yet homespun look, relaxed and unpretentious.

CAREER TIP

Sometimes it is not the food that brings customers back to a restaurant but the dining experience—an environment conducive to social interaction, relaxation, and memorable experiences.

FIGURE 6.10 The interior design of this Maxim's restaurant in Hong Kong is colorful, crisp, contemporary, and inviting. (See color plate 12.)

COFFEE SHOPS

Contemporary coffee shops are a common meeting place for numerous activities. Usually the meetings are composed of small groups. Coffee shops are also a place to work alone using a computer, to read, or to study.

When designing the coffee shop interior, the designer needs to work with more than one type of seating and table configuration. Lounge areas are usually a portion of the seating and traditional tabletops and chairs are another. It is important to understand how heat affects surface materials when selecting tabletops. Coffee and teas also stain surfaces easily so the materials used need to be stain-resistant.

Acoustics are important for these spaces; they are often very small and must accommodate many people having conversations while others try to work quietly.

Convention Centers

Convention centers are often connected to hotels. The size of convention accommodations is related to the size of the hotel. Usually these are large and most often located in major metropolitan or resort areas. Many conventions are planned according to their unique and specific location. Many attendees combine work and vacation, especially if the work event is held at some resort or interesting place.

Convention centers use very aggressive marketing techniques to compete for business. Local chambers of commerce promote convention centers to help with their local economy. Advertising campaigns, e-mail announcements, raffles, and drawings attempt to lure in participants. Because of the size and scope of many conventions, these facilities are usually a boost to the local economy, in addition to promoting whatever products and/or services are being assembled. The facilities need to be adequate for large crowds and flexible in nature due to the various displays, programs, and traffic. They also need to be attention-getting and innovative, usually depending on technology such as speakers, screens, video equipment, sound equipment, and special lighting. Designers can arrange for resources as well as arranging for overall designs, furniture, carpeting, drapery, tables and chairs, and all other necessary equipment.

Convention centers accommodate numerous group sizes. Even in one convention, there are different group or meeting sizes. Large spaces are designed to open up using wall partitions, depending on the function and needed size.

Space planning for convention centers is an area that is prospering and centers' interiors are becoming more user-friendly as opposed to merely being large meeting spaces. Conference centers, in general, can provide comfort and conveniences if properly done. Preconference spaces can be cavernous, cold, and uninviting, but with talented professionals the space can be transformed into a very appropriate and relevant conference site. Build-ups and take-downs need to be simple and safe, using easily transported, yet attractive, materials. Permanent facilities like food courts and cafes, restrooms, registration locations, and ticket areas can provide great design opportunities. Great color combinations, lighting and skylights, floor and wall materials, graphics and art, good traffic patterns, and signage can be selected to make the space comfortable and stylish.

Many businesspeople take advantage of a business convention to take a family vacation. The large facilities and number of additional activities that are typically available encourage family members to go as well. Sometimes the convention center is self-contained with numerous activities and sometimes the convention center is located in a city with many extra activities and attractions.

There may be tourist locations nearby or the center may include attractions as part of the facility: gaming, carnival rides for children, theaters, recreational equipment, indoor and outdoor water parks, ice-skating rinks, and other entertainment facilities. Obviously, the more on-site attractions there are, the more profitable the property can be.

New technology has prompted many convention centers to make necessary changes. Technology also allows for conferencing that does not require participants to be in the same location. These technological advances will undoubtedly change the complexion of conference centers. Teleconferencing equipment, high-tech projection and sound equipment, and retractable walls and ceilings to open up the space are some of the advancements. Building materials are also changing. High-performance textiles, carbon materials, and nanotechnology will change the future of construction.

Conference centers, however, will facilitate destination meetings as long as they remain a tax-effective way to reward employees while getting business done. In looking at the future of conference centers, interior designers could creatively examine new uses for some of these traditional, very large spaces.

FIGURE 6.11 The large space in this convention center is designed for numerous kinds of activities.

Conferencing in general has taken on a new look with new types of furnishings. Traditional tables and chairs are being replaced with lounge seating that accommodates laptop computers, dining, resting, task lighting, and electrical outlets for charging technical equipment.

An informal conference room might have a sectional with a center table that holds drinks and can be written on for note-taking. The notes would then be printed or e-mailed to each participant as required. Multimedia conference rooms are more like theaters.

FIGURE 6.12 This conference room functions for today's technology.

Casinos

Casinos are a growing destination industry. We live in a "something for nothing" society where the chance to win big is thought to be within reach. Most people know at least one person who has "hit the jackpot."

Las Vegas, Nevada, is a destination that was built on gaming and now has something for all ages. Several hotels and casinos even have circus attractions, amusement rides, and activities for every age group.

Many creative people have put together a high-level entertainment environment. Casinos are also home for theater and shows. Interior designers for casinos need expertise in lighting and theater sets. Acoustical expertise is also necessary for both the theaters and multigame areas.

Knowledge of **wayfinding** techniques is also important. Casinos can be very large and within a casino, there are multiple gambling tables, slot machines, bars, and restaurants. All of these can look very similar, which makes wayfinding very important.

Interior designers who have a broad base of expertise for numerous types of commercial interiors can design and coordinate an entire multilevel project, like a casino. In some cases, teams of designers, each with a specific area of expertise, will work together to complete one major interior job.

As a result of the money being made on this type of entertainment, casinos are becoming increasingly popular. Specializing in casino design has many complexities and can easily be a stand-alone target market for an interior designer. It also coordinates well with the hotel and convention industry.

Clubs

Club interior design focuses on country clubs, yacht clubs, golf clubs, tennis clubs, and clubhouse bar, spa, and pro shop facilities. The club interior designer creates a warm, comfortable, and friendly environment that often emphasizes tradition and culture.

Some areas within club design that require custom designs are millwork, bar design, and fireplace mantels. The interior designer will look at current trends for each type of club as well as future trends in each area.

This chapter repeats the importance of acoustics and lighting for all areas, and clubs are no exception. Noise levels need to be controlled with acoustical treatments. The numbers of areas requiring specific lighting are numerous.

Club design can include many **custom** features. Clubs are an opportunity to present custom ideas. Many clubs are very exclusive, thus demanding a unique environment that will entice the elite member.

Interior design professionals need to be very familiar with the activities and characteristics of the desired membership for each type of club. Within clubs, there are spaces for dining, meetings, locker rooms, spa areas, retail sales, and sports bars. The designer can also suggest space usage that might be both unique and desirable.

Chain versus Boutique Design

Especially in the United States, there are many **franchise** businesses. In addition to occupying a certain market niche, they have very consistent menus, products, or "looks;" a great deal of advertising; strong name-recognition; and very specific graphics and logos. The designs of the buildings and interiors are usually very similar if not exactly alike. A designer might be hired to work in all of the various locations, repeating the same design over and over. The public expects and relies upon the familiarity of these businesses. Because of **globalization**, you might find exactly the same restaurant and food in faraway places, all over the globe. The parallels between food and general-merchandise franchises are quite strong, especially in business practices. There are predictable, efficient, and standardized business plans for all outlets.

Boutiques, on the other hand, are very individual and unique, which is one of the main reasons for shopping in one. The merchandise is usually not mass-produced, so you find originality, creativity, and variety in the merchandise and in the interior design.

FIGURE 6.13 The custom details in this private country club interior enhance the club's exclusive character.

Interior Designer Profile 6.1
John Fulton, Vice President of Design and Purchasing, John Q. Hammons Hotels & Resorts, Springfield, Missouri

John Fulton has more than 35 year of hands-on experience in hotel design and purchasing with major hotel corporations. He is currently the president of the International Society of Hospitality Purchasers. He received his bachelor degree in design from the University of Missouri.

"Design management" became a mind-set early on in Fulton's career and continues today. He enjoys the challenge and yet feels comfortable in his job of directing the strategic management of the design and purchasing efforts for an organization that comprises 76 domestic-based hotels—a dozen brands that reach across both full- and limited-service facilities: Renaissance Hotels & Resorts, Marriott Hotels & Resorts, Hilton Hotels, and Holiday Inn Hotels & Resorts, just to name a few.

Fulton is privileged to oversee on a daily basis a talented in-house design team working on new construction, refurbishments, and capital expenditure projects. He also constantly "problem solves" at a fast pace to purchase cutting-edge products at a competitive value. His goal is to maintain a balance of creativity and successful management.

In a corporate setting, skills used daily are planning, evaluating, motivating, calculating, meeting schedules, and working within industry standards to encourage "the team" to successfully complete projects. It also requires strategic planning with suppliers; vendors; manufacturers; architects; project managers; hotel operations staff; chief engineers; in-house legal, accountant, and credit departments; and outside designers and purchasing groups to properly communicate critical details. However, the bottom line is to design and make functional a hotel that is pleasing to the customer—the "guests" at the hotels or restaurants.

Special training is highly important to any successful career. To be competitive in hotel design, you should keep up-to-date with new products and processes. There is value is staying abreast of new materials and developments in such critical design areas as finishes, technology, codes, environmental issues, and industry resources. Within purchasing, it is important to network with manufacturers, suppliers, and other industry professionals.

Possible design careers associated with hospitality and restaurants are architecture; hospitality and restaurant management; procurement; corporate hotel management; construction; office furnishing and other sales; furniture manufacturing; and designing for fabrics, carpets, wall coverings, lighting, and/or furniture.

After 35 years in hotel design and purchasing, Fulton advises designers interested in a career in this area to get involved "early on" with all aspects of a hotel or restaurant—from "back of the house" to marketing and sales. It is imperative to find out how a successful hotel or restaurant functions. From there, you will be able to assimilate what a current facility's functions are, and to then effectively plan the improved processes and creative design that ultimately drive the success of the establishment. This is all a part of getting to know the facility and the ultimate customer—the guest.

SUMMARY

Our eating-out habits and our love of travel and entertainment have created many outlets for the interior designer. Restaurant design sometimes overrides the quality of food. Our desire to experience new things and see new places has been the driving force behind some of the great entertainment venues. Many hotels are visually and culturally significant. Sometimes the economy of adaptive reuse or historical preservation induces the designer to create something very special. Our visual landscape is made up of a huge variety of styles and types of buildings and interiors, reflecting our diverse culture and rich past. Capitalizing on this can inspire the designer and consequently result in some very original places.

RELATED CAREER OPTIONS

- Accessories Dealer
- Acoustic Designer
- ADA Consultant
- Adaptive Reuse Specialist
- Advertising Professional
- Airline Terminals Designer
- Amusement Park Designer
- Antiques Dealer
- Aquarium Designer
- Art Dealer
- Artist
- Auditorium Designer
- Ballrooms Designer
- Bedding Designer
- Boat Designer
- Buyer
- Cabinet and Hardware Designer
- Casino Designer
- Code Specialist
- Commercial Carpet and Flooring Designer
- Communications Designer
- Concert Hall Designer
- Corporate Occasion Designer
- Custom Framer
- Entertainment Center Designer
- Environmental Designer
- Event Designer
- Exhibit Designer
- Floral Designer
- Furniture Designer
- Furniture Restorator
- Graphic Designer
- Green Designer
- Greenhouse and Solarium Designer
- Highway Rest Stop Designer
- Historic Preservationist
- Hospitality Designer
- Hotel Designer
- In-House Corporate Designer
- Landscape Designer
- Mall Designer
- Motel Designer
- Nightclub Designer
- Park Designer
- Publicist
- Real Estate Broker
- Recreation Vehicles Designer
- Restaurant Designer
- Salon Designer
- Set Decorator and Designer
- Spa Designer
- Television Set Designer
- Theater Designer
- Ticketing Outlets Designer
- Transportation Designer

SKILLS AND APTITUDES Qualities needed for a successful career in the hotel, restaurant, and hospitality design field include: creativity; knowledge of business practices; and familiarity with the wants, needs, and tastes of the public. You should have some knowledge of the entertainment and travel industries and should definitely keep up with the latest related products and materials.

EDUCATION A bachelor degree is the best foundation to begin a career in hotel, restaurant, and hospitality, but an associate degree is beneficial as well. Moreover, you can never underestimate the value of great experience—sometimes the best teacher. Many successful hotel, restaurant, and hospitality designers began in the kitchen as dishwashers, then moved up to waiting tables, cooking, and managing; through grit, talent, and determination, they became highly regarded restaurant designers. You will also need to acquire all the experience you can get in the various areas of hospitality, travel, and restaurant services and environments. Study kitchen planning, cooking, space planning, furniture systems, and commercial codes and regulations. There are many other areas of skill necessary; these depend on and are related to each specific area of design.

KEY TERMS

Adaptive Reuse	Franchise	Retro
Ambient Lighting	Globalization	State Codes
Boutique	Historic Preservation	Wayfinding
Custom	Renovation	

DISCUSSION QUESTIONS

1. Discuss the differences between franchise design and boutique design. How does this affect sales?
2. Discuss some original businesses, properties, or entertainment venues that you have encountered. What effect, in your opinion, has the design had on the success of the business?

CHAPTER SEVEN
PRODUCT DESIGN

7

CHAPTER OBJECTIVES After reading this chapter, you should be able to identify and understand the broad spectrum of job opportunities related to product design and product development, including: Furniture • Textiles • Lighting Closet and Storage Products • Art and Accessories • Building Products • New Technology • The Environmental Impact of Product Design • Social Responsibility.

Historical styles, ideas, and traditional products are constantly blended and recycled with new adaptations, applications, and high-tech materials. New designs and innovative ideas for interiors can mean new careers.

The Evolution of a New Product

New products fuel our **consumerism** and provide us with one of our favorite pastimes—shopping. The birth of a new product can originate from one or more sources. Inspiration for a new product can stem from a newly defined need or desire, or even by accident. Regardless, new products keep filling shelves and money keeps changing hands. The starting point for a new product can be a flash of inspiration, a more methodical creative process, or the studious observation of a desire or need. It also originates from new materials or new applications of products.

INSPIRATION

The birth of a new product or design may begin with a fleeting moment of inspiration or an idea that evolved from some need. As that product moves from an intangible idea, through development, and on to the marketplace, it changes hands many times and consequently affects countless people in the workplace—from the inventor or designer to the consumer who selects to use that product in the **built environment.** An entire career or huge business segment could conceivably arise from a single product. It could be a piece of custom-designed furniture that ends up being mass-marketed or a great piece of art that gets mass-produced—a design for a textile that ends up being used in numerous applications. A small stroke of genius can turn into a giant success. What was once a small part of your career can become your career. When Lady Luck smiles, you never know what might happen.

CAREER TIP

Take opportunities to be in beautiful and creative spaces. This could be a garden, a park, or a museum.

The question always arises, does the product drive the market or does the market drive the success of the product? Either way, the interior designer can play a crucial role in the marketplace, and that translates into job opportunity.

Inspiration for a new product can come from many sources. Beauty in nature is often a source and gauge of beauty in the manufactured world. A good designer studies and observes nature: the shapes, forms, colors, light, and the harmony among all these elements of nature. Going to parks, taking nature walks, looking at nature books and pictures, and traveling can bring greater appreciation and inspiration from nature.

FIGURE 7.1 A landscape inspiration.

FIGURE 7.2 Foliage inspired the design of this sofa.

FIGURE 7.3 This furniture was inspired by Chinese architecture.

Historical design often plays an integral role in current design. We look back into history and take those classical, passed-the-test-of-time designs, and adapt, refresh, and manipulate them so they fit the needs, tastes, and materials of today. A good product designer studies art history, goes to museums, and visits historical properties. A knowledge and appreciation of past design provides a foundation on which to create quality design.

PROBLEM SOLVING

Interior design is often problem solving. In finding solutions, new products evolve. Designers solve problems every day and it is in this effort that innovation takes place; the need often sparks the creative thought process. For example, our tabletops are cluttered with remotes of all kinds—from television and DVD controls to gas fireplace or overhead fan devices, to chargers and computer mice, to smart-house controls. A stunning accent table or accessory box, designed to store all these necessary items, would not only be functional, accessible, and offer easy location of these remotes but would also reveal the tabletop.

FIGURE 7.4 Brainstorming with a group of creative people is a fun and useful way to develop new ideas.

CREATIVITY

A creative mind is essential in product development. It is imperative that we look at our surroundings in new ways. With an open mind, we must examine and interpret all that we see—both the details and the "big picture." Look around and pay attention. Creativity can be developed and cultivated. It is not simply some innate talent but one that a designer can nurture and refine. Being creative results in fresh solutions for old problems, and combined with the use of new materials and new applications, unique career paths are inevitably discovered.

> **CAREER TIP**
> Be a creative thinker when solving problems.

CONCEPTUALIZATION TO REALITY

The product idea moves from conception to rough sketches and drawings, to models and other **visualizations.** From there the product becomes reality with the creation of the **prototypes,** or examples. Then the design goes through product and material testing, market testing, production, and finally passes into marketing and distribution. There are numerous levels or segments of product development, each being crucial to the success of the product. Many people have a significant stake in the product's success or failure. Numerous jobs and careers depend on the continual design of new products. Our entire economy depends on the creation of new and better products as our needs and lifestyles change.

FIGURE 7.5 Idea sketches are used for product development.

CAREER TIP Consider new uses for items. Could a piece of furniture such as a headboard be made to look like a handbag with pockets for books, an alarm clock, task lighting, etc.?

The development of new materials and increased technology has expanded product design. The true measure of a product is in its functionality for the intended use, the quality of construction and material, its **life-cycle costing**, and its good design and inherent beauty. We will initially be drawn to a product by its **aesthetics**, how something looks in terms of our perception of beauty. Beauty is truly in the "eye of the beholder," but good design transcends individual taste. The aesthetics of an object involves the manipulation of design principles and elements such as line, color, form, balance, proportion, and texture. A good designer knows the importance of aesthetics, but also realizes that there is so much more than first impressions. The overall look of a product may capture our attention, but in order for us to get the most out of our decorating dollar, we must further evaluate it contingent upon its end use. Is this product going to be durable; is it going to be easy and economical to maintain over the life of the product; and will it have to be replaced quickly? These are life-cycle costing questions that we must ask; otherwise, what might appear to be a good deal could end up costing more per use than something more expensive and of higher quality.

Many of the newer materials used today have improved the overall quality and accessibility of some products. These materials may be easier to maintain, less toxic in our environment, **renewable,** and easier or less costly to produce. Bamboo is one of the most obvious. It is used for many products including hardwood flooring and as a fiber in textiles, accessory items, and furniture. A grass that renews itself rapidly in contrast to trees, bamboo has the strength, dimensional stability, and hardness of oak and needs minimal use of pesticides or fertilization. It is versatile and can be cut various ways. It is sustainable and can be considered "green" to a point. One challenge to bamboo being truly sustainable is that it must often be transported long distances, which is expensive and consumes energy. Consideration of all attributes of a product is essential in order to ensure that product's success.

Careers related to the development stage of products could include designers, **renderers,** software designers and **computer-aided design (CAD)** operators, materials and **performance testers,** researchers, industrial engineers, production managers, and **sourcing** specialists.

THE PRODUCT'S DOWNSTREAM COURSE

Thousands of new products and designs are introduced each year. Many but not all are successful. There are numerous variables that affect the success rate; some are controllable, others are not. The success of a product can be affected by the economy in general, current trends, the scope of advertising and promotion, and even word of mouth. Does the product fill a real or implied need? Does it fill a need or simply a want? Is the product sold in such a manner as to hit the target market? These questions go on and on and the answers dictate the course and inevitable success of a product's development.

A successful product developer studies: the manufacturing process, sourcing of materials, business, marketing, consumerism, and all things related to the marketplace. Visit production facilities and talk to wholesalers and retailers. Study the **globalization** of economies and the import/export of goods. There are many job opportunities and specialties in all of these areas.

MARKETING

Within the marketing segments or phases, there are professionals who push a product even closer to the consumer; these include: **merchandisers,** wholesalers, product representatives, vendors, advertisers, Web designers, and online salespeople. Trade shows, resource venues, design firms, retail shops, and catalogs are some examples of areas that provide marketing job opportunities. With education, sales ability, business and marketing knowledge, and good interpersonal skills, an interior designer can carve out a niche in any one of the market segments. Many manufacturers hire sales representatives to sell and promote products. These reps call on customers, take orders, and have booths at trade shows. An interior designer might work as a merchandiser and set up displays for conferences, or put together store windows in retail shops. A designer with good writing skills might put together ads or develop catalog pages, brochures, or specification sheets. Another marketing tool would be the use of Web pages. A designer with computer and Web page development skills could set pages up for the manufacturer or vendor. The potential for designers in product development and the business world is enormous. It just depends on experience, talent, and desire.

Furniture Design

We attempt, and often succeed, to fill our houses and buildings with functional and serviceable furniture. Ideally, the furniture is artistic and beautiful as well. A furniture design may begin with a simple idea or a design intended for personal use. It may be one of a kind for a special client. The creator of that piece could be an engineer, artist, furniture manufacturer, designer, or an employee or owner of a furniture design firm. Whether the furniture is **custom** or mass-market, the designer or innovator relies on knowing the customers' needs, personal tastes, budgets, and intended use of that product.

Due to advancements in production and technology and the utilization of new materials and finishes, furniture encompasses an ever-changing array of choices. Whether the furniture is for residential or commercial spaces, whether hospitality, institutional, leisure, and so on, the variety is endless. Also, the development of high-tech plastics and high-performance textiles and the expanding use of metals and glass have enabled furniture design to evolve into an enormous outlet for many design careers. Furniture design is not just about classical reproductions, or traditional styling. Furniture design today is about innovation, fashion, progress, and the advancement of art and style through our furnishings.

Furniture design necessitates the study of historical furniture styles, **anthropometrics, ergonomics**, materials, manufacturing, private and public spaces, and cultural variances. There are many career opportunities available to those interested in the furnishing of our homes and businesses.

FIGURE 7.6 Prototypes are the next step to sell an idea.

FIGURE 7.7 This designer is making furniture design selections.

Textiles

The role the textile industry plays in the United States and in the world economy is enormous. Every day, almost everything we encounter has some textile or fiber component, from toothbrushes to transportation, from textiles used in outer space to those found in the depths of the ocean. In large part, the development and continued improvement of manufactured and synthetic textiles have led to hundreds of new uses and new applications. Textiles are used as building components, in medicine, in technology, in art, and in meeting our basic needs in life (e.g., shelter, clothing, protection). Textiles are used to enhance the beauty of our environment as well.

Textiles are essential in our working and living spaces because they can: provide privacy, contribute to temperature regulation, enhance acoustics, dictate style, and be applied practically without limitation for almost everything we use and do. Therefore, the career opportunities in the area of textiles are boundless, and as varied as the applications of textiles.

The meaning of the word *textile* has been expanded to include anything that has fiber as one of its components, whether that fiber is natural or chemical. Obviously, textiles become an integral part of any design career. Jobs related to the textile industry begin at the research level, from concept to creation. Research, fiber production, testing, designing, yarn and textile production, marketing, and merchandising are but a few of the many career opportunities possible in the textile industry. These career possibilities increase exponentially due to the various textile applications.

Textiles pervade every aspect of our lives, but only those directly related to the field of interior design will be discussed in detail.

FIGURE 7.8 Quality control requires several lab tests.

WALL COVERINGS

Many of our wall surfaces, both inside and outside, are covered with textiles—from the felt used for the Mongolian yurt to the finely spun silk covering the walls of an exotic interior. Some of the textiles are used for practical purposes and others purely for aesthetics.

Opportunities for specialization in the area of wall covering depend on the market segment and the intended purpose of these textiles. Manufacturing or designing wall coverings, being a product representative, owning a wholesale or retail establishment, working in a design firm, being an independent interior designer, staffing a resource room, and working in a building materials center are some examples of job opportunities in the area of wall coverings.

FIGURE 7.9 Wall coverings add dimension and enhance interior spaces.

WINDOW TREATMENTS

We cover our windows for many different reasons: privacy, filtering light, eliminating light, insulation, obstructing a view, and decoration. For whatever the purpose, there are many choices available. There are rigid materials and soft materials, generic and specific styles, and materials intended for either inside or outside use. It is the role of the designer to assess the specific needs and come up with a solution for the client. Knowing which materials and textiles work best for specific criteria is essential. There are fabrics, films, shades, blinds, and awnings. There are high-tech treatments that work by remote control. There are treatments encased between the panes of glass and many new solutions for our sometimes complex and elaborate windows.

FIGURE 7.10 Window treatments help to complete as well as soften a room.

Professionals who work with window treatments may design for a **workroom**, where the actual design and construction is done, or may represent a manufacturer or work for a design firm, either residential or contract. Many designers work independently and design custom treatments for individuals or for mass-market production. Historical properties, theaters, businesses, hospitals, hotels, and many other facilities all have the need for appropriate window treatments. Also, the plethora of new textiles has expanded the choices in every category.

FLOOR COVERINGS

Within the textile industry, there are many products for the floor, usually termed **resilient floor materials**, although not all are textiles. Carpeting, rugs, runners, and floor mats are the main categories for textiles used on the floor. We choose floor textiles for texture, acoustics, softness, color and pattern, warmth, delineating space, and many other reasons. The choices of fibers are many: natural, synthetic, woven, tufted, flat, made of piles of various lengths, solid, patterned, and more. The designer chooses the right floor covering based on traffic, the situation, price, whether the space is public or private, and personal preferences.

A designer involved with the development of floor coverings must keep up with the newest products, fiber technology, home and corporate fashion, carpet styling, codes for commercial spaces, and clients' needs. The job opportunities for a designer in the floor covering industry are many; they range from fiber research to designing, manufacturing, marketing, and merchandising. Floor coverings reach the consumer through wholesalers, retailers, design firms, and **independent suppliers.**

FIGURE 7.11 Carpets or area rugs provide definition to a space.

FIGURE 7.12 The upholstery in this airport must meet fire codes and be extremely durable.

UPHOLSTERY

The upholstery segment of the textile industry comprises much more than just textiles for furniture. Although we know that textiles enhance the comfort, appearance, and serviceability of furniture, upholstery is used in transportation vehicles as well. Cars, buses, trains, airplanes, and boats use high-performance textiles that are highly regulated for performance and safety. Upholstery for contract furniture is also tested and regulated.

Much comfort and beauty is added to our interiors by the appropriate use of upholstery. From delicate to indestructible, from simple to complex, upholstery fabrics add color and style to our environments.

The designer understands the technical information and has sufficient product knowledge regarding textiles so as to develop and select the perfect upholstery fabric for the intended situation and furniture style. The job opportunities are many and varied, depending on the market segment.

DOMESTIC FABRICS

Textiles used in the home are many—from the easily observable to those textile components unseen yet present in almost everything we see, touch, and use. The textiles we use in our home need to be functional and appropriate for the intended use, from window treatments, bedding, and carpeting to the building itself. The uses, from practical to aesthetic, provide the designer with an opportunity for creative and innovative solutions to common or unique situations.

INSTITUTIONAL FABRICS

Textiles used in institutional settings are varied, but the regulations and standards are much more stringent than in the category of domestic fabrics. Whether the textiles are used in healthcare, schools, government buildings, or any other public-use building, safety, health, and performance are the most critical concerns involving institutional textiles.

Designers who specialize in textile design and development, especially concerning contract or institutional fabrics, might choose to engage in materials testing, developing product standards, or working for a regulatory body such as the **Federal Trade Commission** or other related groups involved in the textile trade.

FIGURE 7.13 Layers on both beds and windows enhance both design interest and acoustics.

FIGURE 7.14 There are literally thousands of fabrics to select from.

HIGH-PERFORMANCE TEXTILES

New uses in industry, medicine, transportation, building, and technical applications are driving the development of innovative textiles and applications. In the field of medicine, textiles are routinely used in the body for artery repair, shoulder repair, and skin grafting. Textiles are used in outer space, in communications, and in environmental uses. High-performance fibers are used when strength is necessary, in nanotechnology, food packaging, protective gear, and many more areas. Obviously, the opportunity for a specialized career in textiles is enormous and rapidly expanding.

Lighting

Lighting brings life and energy to everything we see in our environment. In addition to illuminating our surroundings, its benefits are both physical and psychological. Without light, we would have no color, activities would be dramatically limited, and our world would not function as we know it. The lack of proper light can have negative psychological implications, such as those experienced by those who suffer from **Seasonal Affective Disorder (SAD)**.

There are many types of lighting: practical, artistic, residential, commercial, workplace-related, recreational, and even some used for medical techniques (e.g., laser and light therapy). Lighting is used for safety, signage, advertising, and dramatic effect in our rooms and buildings. Lighting can be natural or artificial, structural or portable.

The proper use of natural light in our environment can have a substantial effect on our energy usage. It is the responsibility of designers to make use of and manipulate natural light to benefit clients in an environmentally responsible way. After that has been addressed, artificial light is used in an infinite number of ways to fill all lighting needs and wants.

The range of lighting types is enormous and the designer must be familiar with the functions, attributes, costs, amount, and quality of light produced by those types. The design features of the **luminaires** must be evaluated and installation considered. The potential for product design in the area of lighting is as great as it has ever been. The use of high-tech materials, new finishes, advancing technology, and methods of storing solar energy all contribute to career possibilities in product design related to lighting.

There are many specialized areas for lighting designers and licensing available. The American Lighting Association, as discussed in Chapter Nine's "Certified Specialty Areas," provides several levels of certification in lighting design. The opportunity is great for qualified designers to dramatically improve buildings, inside and out, with creative and functional light. Talent, experience, and education give the lighting practitioner the necessary skills to light up our world.

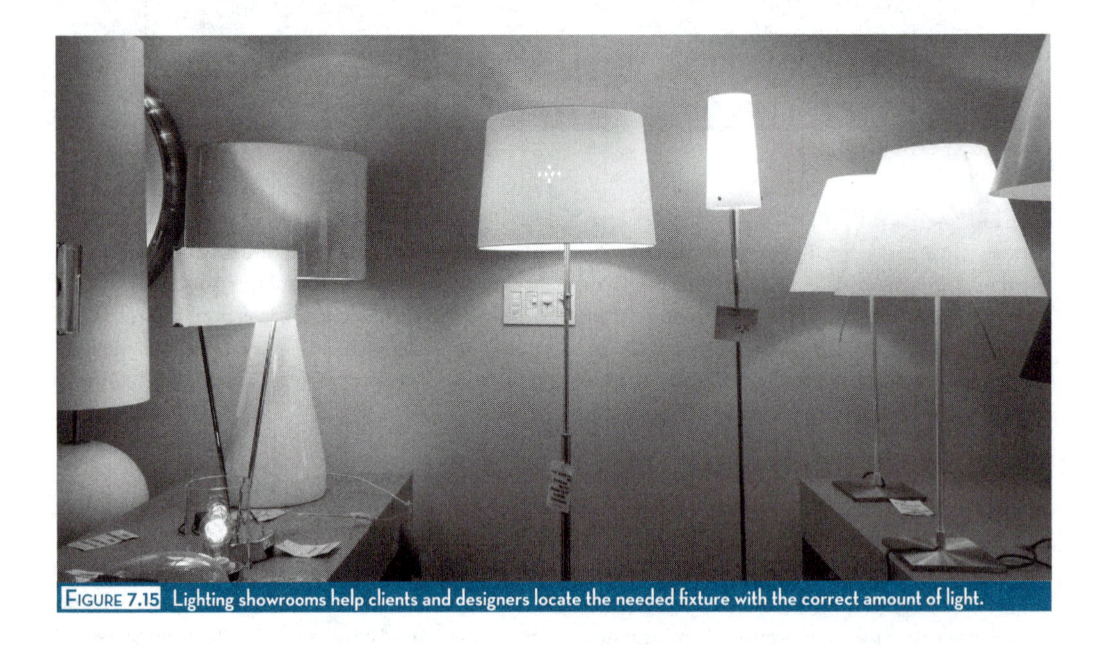

FIGURE 7.15 Lighting showrooms help clients and designers locate the needed fixture with the correct amount of light.

Closet and Storage Products

The efficiency of any space includes products and spaces for storage, including cabinets, closets, shelving, or any other method of storing and organizing our possessions. Storage is even more critical in a commercial or industrial situation; retail stores, production and manufacturing facilities, schools, clinics, and other spaces all have major storage needs. Our need for storage products and design for storage spaces is ever growing as we attempt to organize and declutter our spaces. As we economize and adapt to smaller spaces, whether residential or commercial, we need flexible, multipurpose products for storage.

The product developer needs to have a working knowledge of materials, good organizational skills, spatial acuity, and a familiarity with the particular items to be stored. Training in engineering or **industrial design** would also help prepare one for a career in product development.

Art and Accessories

One of the most creative and expressive areas in product design is that of art and accessories. Every environment requires objects or the use of special materials to give the space character, style, and interest. Artful objects may be the link to tie together all the other elements in a harmonious way. The artistic elements may be structural or decorative, permanent or impermanent, one dramatic piece or more, but in essence, the art and accessories can be the ties that bind. The accessories may be functional as well as artistic.

The designer of art and accessories may be a painter, printmaker, sculptor, fiber artist, woodworker, ceramist, furniture designer, or other type of artist. The work may be mass-produced or custom-ordered. The artist may work independently, for a manufacturing company or a design firm, or sell his or her products through an **art guild.**

The interior designer can be an art and accessories dealer, selling to companies or individuals. An interior designer may specialize in art and accessories, finding the perfect piece for any situation. Whether the designer creates it, finds it, or sells it, the art and accessories can elevate the project in terms of individuality, personalization, uniqueness, and, above all, creativity.

Building Products

Before the designer can begin on any project, a great deal of product knowledge is necessary. From the foot of a building to its highest peak, for residential or commercial, the designer navigates mountains of building products. From the inside to the outside and everything in between, there is one product decision to be made after another. Keeping up with the many new products placed on the market each year is another responsibility of the designer.

Traditional products use both improved materials and new applications for time-tested ones. Product developers continually offer builders, architects, and designers new choices for their projects. The designer needs to be able to evaluate the quality of these new products. Many problems are solved with new products and it is often the problem that initiates the development of a new product. It is our infinite number of choices that gives our built environments the diversity, uniqueness, functionality, and inevitable success of our projects.

New Technology

New technology has changed the way we create products, from automation in the manufacturing plant to the advances that allow us to market products on the Internet. Clients are better informed because of the Internet and other available resources. One of the many roles of the designer is to introduce new products to clients, offering them choices they had not been aware of and ones that were not readily available to them. New products reach the marketplace very quickly due to technology and efficient informational systems. Our world is smaller because of technology, our choices broader, and the responsibilities of the design professional greater than ever before. Staying informed and keeping up with technology is a never-ending process.

Environmental Impact of Product Design

Product development has many facets; one is determining how new products will affect the environment. This involves the choice of materials, the process of production, the necessary resources, transportation, and the eventual disposal of the product; all must be considered. Another concern of the product developer involves how the product could affect **indoor air quality.** What about the use of formaldehyde and other **volatile organic compounds (VOCs)**, vaporous substances that are known carcinogens? Some common products containing VOCs are paint thinners and solvents, formaldehyde, and adhesives. Are the products made from **sustainable** materials? What will be the life-cycle costing of that product? How much energy is used in production, use, and disposal? What about the waste generated during the whole process? Are we using our natural resources to the best of our ability? The environmental concerns of the product developer are serious and affect us in direct and not-so-direct ways.

Another thing to consider is a system that will recycle products and promote the reuse, repair, renovation, restoration . . . and the list of R's goes on and on. The product developer has a responsibility to the public to be resourceful and conscientious, and to protect the health and safety of the consumers who use the products.

Social Responsibility

The product developer needs to incorporate the guidelines established by the **ADA** when applicable. The best and most successful designs accommodate the needs of both its specific users and the general public. Products created with **universal design** as the basic criteria also increase the number of potential users of those products. It is not only socially responsible to create products that are easy to use by everyone but it is good for sales as well.

The numbers of special-needs users continue to increase, whether due to disability or because of aging. The high percentage of older citizens dictates the need for easy-to-use, practical, functional, and affordable products. A successful product developer is also aware of cultural differences. The needs and wants of different cultural groups should broaden the range of product choices. Preserving the richness of cultural differences is important, and respective ethnic products enable us to do that. Our marketplace is a world rich in design, style, and color and the choices are many.

INTERIOR DESIGNER PROFILE 7.1
Jeff M. Walker, Technical Designer and Product Developer, BridgeBlue Sourcing Partners, LLC, Springfield, Missouri

Jeff M. Walker is on the fast track to success. He graduated from Missouri State University in 2006 and is currently working on his MBA in project management and LEED certification, having passed the NCIDQ examination. Walker is proficient in Autodesk, Auto-CAD, Revit, Photoshop, and SketchUp. He is an allied member of ASID, the Home Builders Association of Greater Springfield, and the Springfield Design Association.

Why have you specialized in product design?

I love designing, period. Product development is unique because it is most always function-driven design that utilizes an extremely broad range of materials and processes. In any given day I can be involved in the designs for high-end pet saunas, outdoor fire pits, a Queen Anne–style console, or a set of contemporary candlesticks. It's that kind of rapid change of pace that makes this particular design field so challenging, and yet so exciting!

What has contributed to your fast track to success?

I consider myself successful only because I set high professional goals and strive to achieve them by any means possible throughout my career—although the goals are constantly changing and almost never am I able to complete what I had set out to originally complete.

Success is not about money. I drafted for a company making a more significant amount of money prior to taking the position in development, but the challenge and the feeling that every day is something new makes the job worthwhile. I consider anyone successful who, one, enjoys what they do every day for a living, and, two, constantly pursues making that thing they do every day better in some small way.

How do you get inspired for product design?

I take inspiration for my designs from travel abroad, fashion, and interior design trends as well as historical reference, natural surroundings, and countless other design stories that abound all around us every day. The real key to good product design is tailoring the look that you want to the look that would fit into your target customer's home or business, while also convincing the buyer of that same goal. This can take you to some very interesting places design-wise. For instance, a recent project had me designing a circus-themed birdcage as a candleholder. That's proof-positive that anything can serve as inspiration when you are designing product[s]!

What other types of design are you interested in?

I'm foremost a "technical designer." What I mean by that is that I love function-driven design. I love to take an initial product concept and figure out how it would be built the best, detailing every nut, bolt, screw, material, finish, and quality control. I currently help to design accent furniture, accessories, and lighting, as well as high-end pet products for some of the nation's largest retailers. I've always wanted to expand my expertise to include custom high-end interior lighting. Lighting design/consulting would be a dream job of mine, and had it been an option to focus on at the university I went to, I would have signed up immediately. It is definitely something that I'll be pursing at some point in my career.

What are your goals as an interior designer? Where do you see yourself going professionally?

I've set many goals, professionally speaking. I have a dedication to increasingly incorporating at least a small amount of sustainability into every design I am involved in. Other goals include continual education and lifetime learning advances. This includes a specific intent to study new methods and materials, sharpening my knowledge on existing methods to better design from. It is so very important to me as an interior or product designer to know the processes involved in a design. For example, knowing and anticipating the way that a resin mold will react to an intricately patterned design is crucial. Likewise, anticipating how concrete would react when used in a custom reception desk design can greatly impact the successful execution of a design job. I eventually see myself involved with interior design legislation and/or education. A very strong passion of mine is helping others come to an elevated level of learning and excitement in their careers!

How did you prepare for the NCIDQ exam? Do you think your education adequately prepared you for it or was it your experience, or both, and in what proportions?

I used every reference I could find to prepare for the NCIDQ exam. I fretted and studied for months! In the end, I realized that professional on-the-job experience is the single most important factor in preparing effectively for an exam of that type. When you are on the job, just ask about everything that you can possibly ask about. Ask why that piece of wood has to be $\frac{1}{4}$-inch and not $\frac{1}{8}$-inch thick. Ask why that carpet needs to look like that or be red rather than blue in a particular space. Put yourself out there and learn all you can. There is no better way to learn and grow. Education will almost always come in the doing, more than in the reading and writing.

What advice do you have for aspiring interior designers?

My advice to anyone considering or pursuing placement in the field would be simple. Never accept a standard as it is written or expected. Always strive to do better than any standard requires of you! In doing such, you overcome mediocrity; take yourself to a higher level of learning and personal achievement, and maybe (just maybe!) design something new and inspiring! People take notice in you more when you are different. The best way to be different is to go above and beyond. In short, do your best and it will eventually happen—almost always.

SUMMARY

The product developer can take many career paths and specialize in many areas, from the initial idea and first sketch to the delivery of the product into the consumer's hands. Product developers are problem solvers. Product developers are creative individuals who are educated, concerned about the environment, and sensitive to the needs of all people.

RELATED CAREER OPTIONS

- Acoustic Designer
- ADA Consultant
- Adaptive Reuse Specialist
- Advertising Professional
- Art and Accessories Dealer
- Artist
- Cabinet and Hardware Designer
- Carpet and Floor Material Designer
- Catalog Designer
- Colorist
- Communications Designer
- Cost Estimator
- Custom Framer
- Custom Window Treatment Designer
- Domestic Textile Designer
- Energy Conservationist
- Furniture Designer
- Graphic Artist
- Industrial Designer
- Lighting Analyst
- Manufacturer
- Manufacturer's Representative
- Market Researcher
- Materials Specialist
- Model Designer
- Packaging Designer
- Paint Manufacturer
- Product Buyer
- Production Manager
- Textile Conservator
- Textile Designer
- Textile Historian
- Trend Forecaster
- Universal Designer
- Workroom Owner

SKILLS AND APTITUDES The skills and aptitudes of the product developer are many. A developed eye for detail, an innovative mind, and the ability to solve problems are among the many necessary aptitudes. An individual able to discern good design, look to the future, and listen to the wants and needs of the public will have the required assets for a product designer. Some of the skills necessary, depending on which stage of product development one engages in, have to do with: production methods, equipment usage, conceptual drawings, construction, and knowledge of materials.

EDUCATION With a bachelor degree or an associate degree in interior design, an individual will have enough overall design knowledge relative to interior environments to get a head start with any career related to product design. Technical schools offer classes and certification in specific areas including construction and manufacturing. These types of educational opportunities can be obtained before a four-year college or university program or come sometime after as further education. There are excellent art and design schools for those interested in this type of design. As always, education provides a strong foundation for experience.

KEY TERMS

- Aesthetics
- Americans with Disabilities Act (ADA)
- Anthropometrics
- Art Guild
- Built Environment
- Computer-Aided Design (CAD)
- Consumerism
- Custom
- Ergonomics
- Federal Trade Commission
- Globalization
- Independent Supplier
- Indoor Air Quality
- Industrial Design
- Life-Cycle Costing
- Luminaires
- Merchandisers
- Performance Testers
- Prototype
- Renderers
- Renewable
- Resilient Floor Materials
- Seasonal Affective Disorder (SAD)
- Sourcing
- Sustainable
- Textiles
- Universal Design
- Visualization
- Volatile Organic Compound (VOC)
- Workroom

DISCUSSION QUESTIONS

1. Discuss how a perceived need transforms into the development of a product.
2. Do you see dramatic changes in our product choices based on our environmental concerns?
3. Discuss whether public demand leads to product development or product developers create perceived needs in the minds of the consumer.

CHAPTER EIGHT
OPPORTUNITIES FOR SPECIALIZATION

8

CHAPTER OBJECTIVES

After reading this chapter, you should be able to: Think more creatively about **specialization** opportunities in interior design • Understand how specialty areas can be developed • Critically consider why specialization is important to the interior design professional.

The interior design profession is for creative people. Traditionally, interior designers work with a client from the initial interview through the completion of the job. An interior design job can be extremely rewarding for everyone involved or it can be very frustrating for everyone. The difficulty comes with the number of aspects of a project that are out of the control of the interior designer and the client.

It is the interior designer's responsibility to inform and communicate clearly and regularly with his or her client. The interior designer and the client need to clearly identify what group of people will participate and the responsibilities of those people. Which companies will be involved to provide goods and other services? Who will do the plumbing and the electricity, the carpet installation, and the framing? Where will the building material, the windows, and the roofing material come from? The lists go on. The interior designer will assign and depend on experts in all the **subcontracted** areas of an interior design project. Depending on experts in a particular field is critical. Money is a driving force that can misdirect designers into areas that are best left up to other experts. There are not enough hours in the day to be completely involved in all aspects of interior design projects. An exception to this is when a designer works on only one or two jobs at a time. However, it is best to rely on allied professionals for their expertise and experience. **Allied professionals** include contractors, plumbers, electricians, framers, and other experts in their respective fields. A designer

FIGURE 8.1 CAD projects are very time-consuming and can be a great specialty area.

FIGURE 8.2 This workroom produces custom projects for a number of interior design professionals.

cannot possibly know everything about everything, so you work cooperatively with those professionals who can contribute their expertise. A good designer knows his or her limitations, but finds solutions or allied professionals to do their part to ensure a successful project. You, as a professional creative person, may be either the primary interior designer in charge of a project or that specialized expert called in to consult on a particular area of design. In either case, it is important to consider the many opportunities for specialization.

Create a Specialty for More Income

As the interior design professional has become more recognized in our society, so have many types of specialty areas in the field of interior design. Designers are zeroing in on areas of projects and specific types of jobs where their talents and interests can thrive. Often, this can create the most income.

Specialization can be:

- An isolated segment of the interior design project, such as **computer-aided design (CAD), project managing,** or **drapery fabricating.**
- A special style or a specific area of design.
- Specific areas within an interior, such as a kitchen and bath or a restaurant and lounge.
- A specific type of business, such as hotels or hospitals.
- A style, such as *traditional* or *contemporary.*
- A type of building, such as a home or business.

Because completing an interior design project involves numerous projects, more and more areas of specialization are turning up.

Components of an Interior Design Project

Components of an interior design project include: sales and marketing (how the job will be acquired), **programming** (what the job will entail), interior design decisions, and interior design presentations that often include formal **presentation boards** and/or computer-generated presentations. A mountain of paperwork accompanies almost every interior design project; this includes time sheets, **material and finish schedules**, and purchase orders for all aspects of a job. Selections for floors, walls, ceilings, doors, and windows must be documented. **Furnishing specifications; fixtures schedules** for plumbing items; **fabrications** of cabinetry, drapery, and window treatments; and special designs such as mantels or custom furnishings must be arranged. **Receiving**, installations, plans for outdoor spaces, and supervision of all of the above must be accomplished. Programming for **time lines**, from conception through completion, must be developed.

Many interior design–related areas have potential for an independent business segment or an income-producing specialty of their own. The key to making money in any of these specialties is expertise and business volume. The business volume will follow with enough attention given to an area of expertise.

Business Practices

Interior designers should also rely on experts in their field. An example of this is accounting. Business practices are an area that interior designers many times ignore or do not devote enough time to. The business part of interior design is not creative enough for some designers. A professional accountant often best handles important details such as collecting deposits, determining design fees, and paying for all of the business-related expenses. The business of interior design is similar to other businesses and record-keeping is time-consuming. Keeping the money and financial obligations organized is important for profit, maintenance, and expanding a business. Interior designers who also have a degree in business can specialize in this area for other interior design professionals. Specialized business professionals who are also designers would better understand interior designers and the way they work.

Residential and Commercial Specialties

As we have seen from Chapters Two and Three, "Residential Interior Design" and "Commercial Interiors," basic specialty areas are commercial and residential. Residential interior designers often work out the entire scope of services and business-related aspects with their clients. The size of a home is typically not so overwhelming that, with a reasonable amount of time, a designer can't successfully design, present, complete all specifications for, order all products for, and supervise the job.

Fabrication and installation of products and materials are not usually included in the average scope of services carried out by the designer in charge of the project. Interior designers work on numerous projects simultaneously. In addition to fabrication and installations, residential interior designers are most likely to seek specific help in the areas of kitchen and bath,

CAREER TIP

Be familiar with the many available computer programs for drawing and presentation.

custom cabinetry, communications systems, and landscaping. Professionals who specialize in these areas can be consulted when working on these projects.

Residential interior designers do not always have adequate time to handle some areas of the design. Areas that often become opportunities for other professionals to specialize in include: window treatment fabrication, upholstery, **slipcovers**, table linens, bed covering fabrication, wall covering installation, painting and finishing walls and ceilings, furniture, and landscaping. Specialty areas like these become business opportunities for other interior designers. Each product that is used to complete an interior design job involves someone who knows and sells the idea and products to the interior designer who is in charge of that project.

CAREER TIP

Interior designers have favorite "systems" companies. The open office system they know most about will mostly likely be their favorite—this will be the one they most often specify because it's their specialty.

If there is a specific type of product that interests a designer, the sales and marketing of that product can be very rewarding. This is an opportunity to spend time on what some designers find most enjoyable.

SALES REPRESENTATIVES

There are **sales representatives** for every product and they keep the designers informed. Fabric sales representatives, for example, can be interior designers who enjoy fabric, sales, and traveling. Interior designers in specific product areas communicate well with professionals because of their similar background. Product sales are increased with an understanding of products, an outgoing personality, and interior design experience. Sales representatives are needed for all interior design products, such as flooring, wall coverings, furniture, lighting, and accessories.

WINDOW TREATMENTS

Window treatments that are not drapery, such as blinds, shades, or shutters, provide another opportunity for interior designers. Blinds are available in both vertical and horizontal styles. Within each style are hundreds of sizes, fabrics, metals, plastics, composites, and paints. Shades are available in the traditional roller style as well as many new contemporary horizontal and vertical styles. Some companies specialize only in shutters of all sizes, usually in a variety of wood types and composite materials that are stained or painted.

WORKROOMS

Interior designers who enjoy working with fabric have opportunities to own and operate a drapery **workroom**, an upholstery shop, a custom slipcovers shop, or create custom linens. All of these areas require knowledge in precision-sewing as well as knowledge in the specific area of custom work. Many interior designers in both commercial and residential fields use all of these services. Workrooms of this nature usually provide employment for a number of interior designers. Some large furniture companies have all these fabricating workrooms **in-house** for only their clients. Controlling these additional profit centers is great when a company has enough trained professionals and a large enough volume of business to keep all areas in production.

There are many companies that offer numerous custom fabric finishes and treatments such as paper backing (for wall covering), flameproofing, adding vinyl finishes, and making roller shades. There are other companies that put edging or fringe on area rugs, and make custom pillows, place mats, table runners, chair covers, or slipcovers for couches. Whatever the need, there is someone to provide the service.

ALTERNATIVE RESIDENTIAL INTERIORS

Housing for the elderly is becoming more prevalent with our aging population. Within this specialty area are apartments for the elderly, independent living that includes community services such as dining and organized activities, and full-care nursing facilities. Several of these living situations include on-site services such as grooming salons and shopping. Nursing facilities are covered in Chapter Four, "Healthcare."

Universal design is a result, again, of our aging population and offers another opportunity for specialization. Universal design means design that works for everyone, regardless of special needs. It deemphasizes the separation of the special-needs population from the population as a whole.

Cynthia Leibrock is a well-known expert, speaker, and author who writes about universal design. She has written many books and articles, two of which are *Design Details for Health: Making the Most of Interior Design's Healing Potential* and *Beautiful Universal Design, a Visual Guide.* Writing about areas in interior design is an opportunity for specialization and usually includes speaking engagements. It will be discussed below.

COMMERCIAL SPECIALTIES

Commercial interiors can be divided into healthcare, commerce, hospitality, restaurant, retail, religious, educational, government, and general office space. Under each of these specialties are additional opportunities to focus in one particular area. Commercial interiors in general are discussed in Chapter Three, "Commercial Interiors," while healthcare, as previously stated, is discussed in Chapter Four.

All facilities have products and issues that are unique to their design and function. Banks, for example, have vaults, privacy issues, security systems, and a strong, safe, secure interior environment. In the category of financial, or commerce, are banks, savings and loans, mortgage companies, and investment corporations.

Hospitality includes hotels, motels, and resorts. Restaurants can be a stand-alone structure or included in other facilities such as hotels, retail, or healthcare spaces. Chain restaurants usually work with an interior designer who makes the decisions for all their locations.

Retail interior design can be **window design** along with store and display design. It can also be only store design or only window design. Retail can be one company or a major chain store that provides interior design for all their property locations.

Religious interior design is sometimes a company that specializes in selling church seating and symbolic items and furnishings, and includes all necessary products such as carpet, wall coverings, lighting, and general office furnishings appropriate for spaces of worship.

Educational interior design is for a school building or a campus of buildings. Budgets for designing educational spaces are usually a priority along with function and maintenance. Government interior design sometimes includes education.

SPECIAL PRICING

Special pricing exists for certain groups. This pricing is well-established and clearly defined. It is not pricing for the general public or quantity pricing, but a category in itself. It would apply only to government property or nonprofit organizations.

A unique part of interior design for government buildings is the pricing structure for products sold. At the federal level, there is **General Services Administration (GSA)**. The GSA negotiates prebid contracts for office furniture so that each agency knows exactly the negotiated price of products. This process is reviewed every year to ensure the best possible pricing. Interior design fees and other service fees such as installation are not included in GSA pricing. At the state level, state contracts are used. These are also prebid for furniture only and reviewed and extended from year to year. City and county contracts have more flexibility. The furnishings are put out to bid as needed or contracts with specific furniture companies can be negotiated.

State, city, county, and other nonprofit entities also use what is titled the **U.S. Communities' Master Intergovernmental Cooperative Purchasing Agreement.** Not all major companies are on this contract because it is reserved for nonprofit organizations. The special pricing on all of these types of contracts is usually much more competitive than on nongovernmental projects.

Working with government interior design and office furnishings also requires specific budgetary knowledge in order to help each specific agency use the entire allocated budget per **spending period.** In government interior design it is important to maintain a close working relationship with the **purchasing agent** at each location. Those in charge of purchasing typically are aware of the jobs within the agency that are next in line for a redesign or new design project. If an interior designer has a business that is located in a state capital, city government interior design is an opportunity for specialization.

INTERIOR DESIGN FOR GENERAL OFFICE SPACE

General office interior design includes all other commercial buildings and facilities. This includes the corporate office space for numerous businesses. Corporate offices can be designed with the occupant in mind instead of relying on generic choices. These personal offices can be designed for the individual, can sometimes be high-end in costing, and can be very reflective of success. The same interior designer who is in charge of the executive's home interior sometimes does these offices.

Within general office spaces, private offices are sometimes designed separately by a designer who is not in charge of the general office space. Interior design professionals can easily work together as long as the scope of services is clearly outlined for all the interior design professionals and the building or business owner. Another example of more than one interior designer on a project is when one interior designer makes the selections and specifications and another interior designer or designers are responsible for providing the necessary products for the job. Provided that all jobs are clearly defined, this can also produce very successful results.

CHANGING NEEDS ADD SPECIALTY OPPORTUNITIES

The way that business is done is ever-changing, and these changes provide new areas for specialties in interior design. Home offices are more common. Outdoor spaces, both residential and commercial, are making living and working environments more pleasant.

Private and semiprivate small spaces within and around buildings are sought after as a place to meet or take a break from routine activities. Many times these spaces are designed for one or two people and need to accommodate technology (e.g., personal computer use including Internet access) and places for a drink, snack, chair massage, or even a nap.

Coffee shops, located practically everywhere, are one of the recent new business places to meet outside the office. This may be the place of choice to work privately on a personal computer, to interview a client or potential employer or employee, or to have a small meeting with four or fewer people.

Another opportunity for specialization is small spaces and coffee shop facilities enclosed within another type of space. Small coffee shops inside a library, bookstore, supermarket, or corporate office building are good examples. Small places or small private-space design could also require product design to accommodate these specific areas, sizes, and activities.

Call centers for many types of businesses are a growing part of our economy. People can purchase most any product via the Internet. This requires various sizes of call spaces depending on the volume of calls for the product or products. These call centers can accommodate many employees with lots of communications equipment. Acoustic control is important because of the specific type of work. Customer service departments of product companies, banks, credit card companies, IT companies, political offices, survey companies, marketing groups, or any other type of business that requires telecommunication as its main service would benefit by having a call center. Growing numbers of businesses are **outsourcing** these centers. It is common to hear a foreign accent on the phone when checking on an order or when receiving any kind of telemarketing call. Credit card companies, for example, have call centers to accommodate everyday business.

FIGURE 8.3 Designing call centers for numerous part-time workers who need privacy and interaction with coworkers is a space planning challenge.

FIGURE 8.4 Haworth products feature numerous office solutions.

Call centers require open, flexible, acoustically semiprivate spaces with small work and computer spaces. **Open office planning** is the required interior design expertise required for this work. **Systems furnishings** are used for open office planning. Interior designers who work with this space planning are typically marketing a specific brand of furnishings, such as Haworth, Herman Miller, Kimball, or Steelcase. There are more than one hundred systems manufacturers on the market; however, these are some of the top companies in the industry.

Open office designing using systems furnishings is also common in other spaces that require small, open working areas and flexibility. The cost of **reconfiguring** a system is considerably less than moving constructed walls. The time saved in reconfiguring a furniture system is also a consideration.

Another opportunity for specialization is **total office** system design. Some office furniture and systems companies have the capabilities to totally construct an office to attach to a foundation. These companies install all the plumbing, heating, air-conditioning, electrical, walls, doors, windows, ceiling, roofing, and necessary open office furnishings as part of a flexible, movable, and **tax-deductible equipment package**. Most office systems companies now offer floor-to-ceiling partitions, interior doors, and windows in addition to general office partitions. Open office systems vary in height, from desk-height with no privacy to sitting- and standing-privacy.

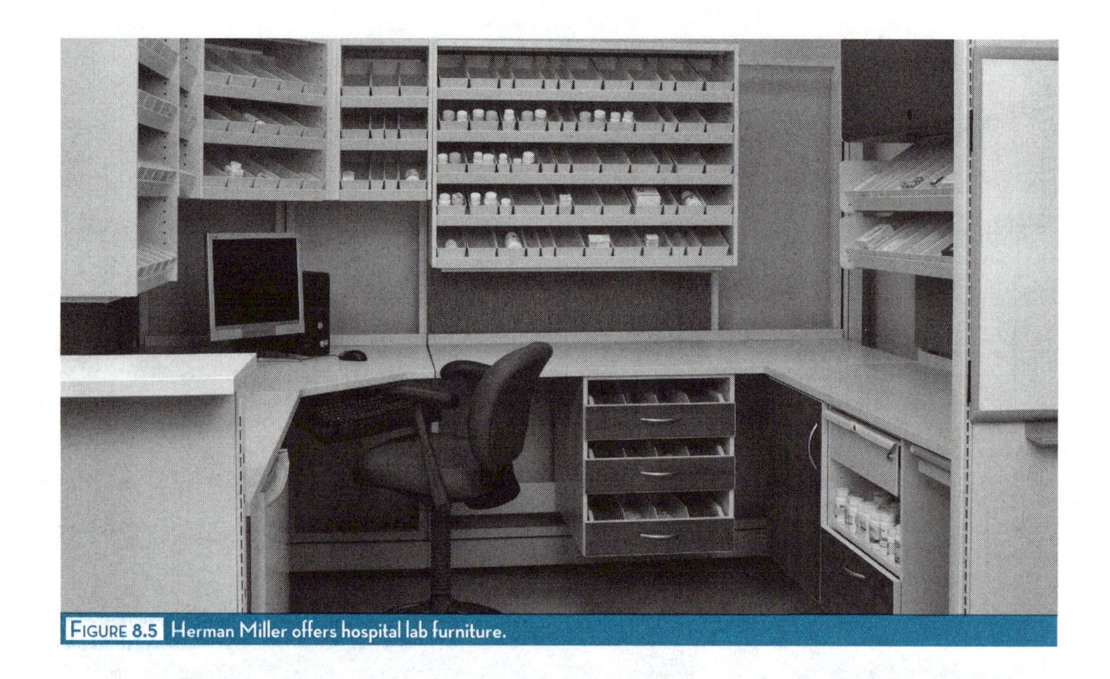

FIGURE 8.5 Herman Miller offers hospital lab furniture.

FIGURE 8.6 Steelcase conference furnishings offer up-to-date solutions.

ART AND ACCESSORIES

Both commercial and residential interior design requires art and accessories. **Art brokering** can be another opportunity for specialization. Most art brokers represent numerous artists and practically any type of art object and work closely with interior designers to select art that enhances each project.

Art brokers who are also interior designers have a great advantage in understanding the needs and design elements for a job. Brokers who provide the service of installing the art and accessories have an extra advantage that is very helpful to the project interior designer and the client.

HOLIDAY DESIGNS

Holiday designs are a business opportunity. Both commercial and residential spaces usually decorate for at least one holiday. It can be a great relief to have a creative person such as an interior design professional enhance the available space per holiday, doing both the installation and the removal of all decorations.

This would also allow the holiday designs to vary from year to year, generating more interest, uniqueness, and excitement. With proven, satisfied clients, business would expand both in the number of holidays requiring decorations and in the number of clients requesting them.

FIGURE 8.7 Elaborate holiday decor is very labor-intensive for homeowners.

FIGURE 8.8 Holiday designs for commercial spaces are best when left up to an outside source.

CAREER TIP Descriptive company names emphasize specialties. Some examples are: Custom Holiday Designs, Workroom Works, and Outdoor Spaces.

WRITING ABOUT INTERIOR DESIGN

Writing for and about interior design is a career opportunity. Magazines, newspapers, books, and special types of publications are constantly publishing reports and other types of writing about interior design. Articles are written about unique spaces; issues in interior design, such as accreditation and licensing; and industry awareness. Articles are written about new interior-related ideas and products, and there are frequently showcase reporting, such as reports about the homes of the rich and famous, and weekly home features that appear in many newspaper publications. Authoring books of design-related subjects, even textbooks for interior design, are part of this specialization. If one has great writing skills and an interest in interior design, writing for a magazine or authoring books is a wonderful career choice.

Writing for interior design also involves marketing and the advertising of interior design firms. Communications, a field that relies heavily on the written word, could be a separate department in a large interior design or architectural firm. An advertising company might also designate an office or desk for interior design communications—promotional materials, ads, catalog entries, and descriptions of products and designs—as well.

OUTDOOR DESIGN

Interior design is extending rapidly to include outdoor spaces that require design ideas similar to those of the interior space. Patio furnishings have expanded to include elaborate outdoor kitchens, fireplaces and fire pits, and dining and outdoor-living furniture. Many companies provide a large selection of outdoor furniture, fabrics, and area rugs.

This area of interior design works well with landscape design. Landscape design is an area of expertise that, combined with an interior design degree, would offer another profitable design opportunity. An interior designer and a landscape architect could work together to provide design ideas and products for outdoor living spaces.

INTERIORS FOR TRANSPORTATION

Transportation provides numerous opportunities for specialization. Cruise ships, airline companies, and the automobile industry all have interiors to be designed. These companies sometimes have their own interior designers on staff and sometimes hire independent designers or firms.

FIGURE 8.9 Outdoor space is a pleasant addition to the available living area.

Image of the Interior Designer

An interior design career can be a very romantic notion. Television reality shows, numerous interior design publications, and public perception have all helped romanticize this career. It's a career that has lots of people around the perimeter who have talent and a genuine interest in interior design, but it is the educated designer who has the knowledge and experience to successfully get the job done.

Through education, experience, and keeping abreast of the new products, materials, and customer demands, the designer needs to be a lifelong learner. There are trade shows to attend, periodicals and books to read, and clients to keep in touch with by listening to their needs and wants. The formal education begins at school, whether a community college, university, art and design school, or any other type of diploma program. On-the-job training is also part of the education/experience and can run concurrently with formal education or begin after the coursework is completed. The two- or four-year study is just the beginning of a lifetime of learning, but when you can directly apply that knowledge, learning is automatic and motivating. Interior design is ever-changing and that is exactly what makes it fascinating, never dull, and never static. Each client and each project affords a new opportunity for learning. New challenges are what engage the creative spirit.

FIGURE 8.10 The luxury of a cruise is definitely reflected in the interior design of the ship.

Specializing for Profit

The interior design profession has hundreds of related products, skills, and avenues that are opportunities for specialization. Interior designers, interior decorators, and interior architects are all very popular artistic career directions. Often, specializations are chosen from a need to make more money because an expert in any field can charge accordingly.

Everyone has heard of the starving artist. A major challenge for artistic professionals is making money. Working efficiently, specializing in what a designer does best, understanding business practices and how money can be made, and knowing which products and services are profitable can enable the designer to become very successful. Specialization, in many cases, has become not only an important part of the interior design career but a necessary one.

Specialists in interior design have also made traditional interior designers' businesses prosper by offering additional help and expert product knowledge. The numerous specialists in interior design help all related professionals look more professional.

Interior Designer Profile 8.1

Beverly McAuley, Sales Representative, Kansas City, Missouri, Edelman Leather, LLC, New Milford, Connecticut

Beverly McAuley has a bachelor of science degree in interior design from Kansas State University. She did her internship with a commercial interior design firm. Seeing tough economic times after graduation, McAuley decided to start her own company. She literally went door to door creating clients and created a successful business.

When the opportunity came for an interior design position with a high-end division of a kitchen and bath company, she started a new career once again. Through the process of learning to sell kitchen and bath products, she became familiar with the local design community.

With her kitchen and bath contacts, McAuley had the opportunity to sell stone and tile. She worked as a sales representative in this industry for ten years.

She became aware of the fact that interior designers could not possibly know everything about all products.

When a sales position became available with Edelman Leather, LLC, she changed positions. Now she truly enjoys working with Edelman Leather. Edelman focuses on design and custom work.

McAuley suggests picking your products wisely. Product lines are very different. Some are more focused on custom design. Others are focused on bottom-line sales. Find your comfort zone.

She believes that designers should work in the design field first and then go into sales. Companies almost always look for those interior designers who have design experience.

While working for an interior design firm, get to know the sales reps who call on you. With these acquaintances, designers will learn of products and job openings that may interest them.

Decorators usually charge less than interior designers.

SUMMARY

The benefits of specializing in a particular area of interior design, whether it is your whole business or just a fraction of it, can be worth the additional education and experience. The rewards can be both financial and personal. There is an increase in credibility when you specialize and earn certification or licensing in a particular area, and with that comes additional professional respect and profit.

RELATED CAREER OPTIONS

- Acoustic Designer
- ADA Specialist
- Adaptive Reuse Specialist
- Advertising Professional
- Airline Terminal Designer
- Amusement Park Designer
- Antiques Dealer
- Aquarium Designer
- Architectural Space Planner
- Art and Accessories Dealer
- Artist
- Auditorium Designer
- Author
- AutoCAD Specialist
- Ballroom Designer
- Bedding Designer
- Boat Designer
- Buyer
- Cabinet and Hardware Designer
- Carpet and Flooring Designer
- Children's Spaces Designer
- City Planner
- Civil Drafter
- Code Specialist
- Colorist
- Commercial or Industrial Designer
- Communications Designer
- Computer Software Engineer
- Concert Halls Designer
- Construction Firm Owner
- Contract Designer
- Cost Estimator
- Curator
- Custom Framer
- Custom Window Treatments Designer
- Design Consultant

- Design Contractor
- Designer for Corporate Occasions
- Designer for Places of Worship
- Detention Facilities Designer
- Development Model Designer
- Educational Facilities Designer
- Educator
- Energy Conservationist
- Entertainment Center Designer
- Environmental Designer
- Event Designer
- Event Planner
- Exhibit Designer
- Facilities Manager
- Faux Finisher
- Feng Shui Specialist
- Fireplace Designer
- Floral Designer
- Funeral Designer
- Furniture Designer
- Furniture Restorator
- Furniture Retail Salesperson
- Gallery Owner
- Governmental Designer (City, State, and Federal)
- Graphic Designer
- Green Designer
- Greenhouse and Solarium Designer
- Healthcare Designer
- Highway Rest Stop Designer
- Historic Preservationist
- Hospitality Designer
- In-House Corporate Designer
- Institutional Designer
- Journalist
- Kitchen and Bath Designer
- Landscape Designer
- Lighting Analyst
- Loft Specialist
- Mall Designer
- Manufactured Housing Specialist
- Manufacturer's Representative
- Market Researcher
- Merchandise Displayer
- Model Creator
- Nightclub Designer
- Outdoor-Living Designer
- Packaging Designer
- Paint Manufacturer
- Park Designer
- Photographer
- Project Manager
- Property Manager
- Publicist
- Real Estate Broker
- Recreational Vehicles Designer
- Renderer
- Residential Consultant
- Restaurant Designer
- Retail Designer
- Retail Salesperson
- Sales Representative
- Salon Designer
- Set Decorator
- Set Designer
- Showroom Designer
- Spa Designer
- Space Planner
- Sports Arena Designer
- Staging Specialist
- Stairway Designer
- Stencil Designer
- Technical Supporter for CAD
- Television Set Designer
- Textile Designer
- Theater Designer
- Ticketing Outlets Designer
- Tile Designer
- Transportation Designer
- Trend Forecaster
- Universal Designer
- Upholsterer
- Visual Merchandiser
- Window Designer
- Workroom Owner

SKILLS AND APTITUDES The skills and aptitudes necessary to be successful in any of the specialized areas are very similar to the ones that any interior designer possesses. The focus only becomes more direct and further exploration is necessary in the respective area.

EDUCATION A bachelor degree is preferred, but an associate degree provides a good base as well, along with additional education in the chosen specialized area. In some areas of expertise, certification or licensing may be available. See Chapter Nine, "Certified Specialty Areas," for more information on special licensing.

KEY TERMS

- Allied Professionals
- Art Brokering
- Call Center
- Computer-Aided Design (CAD)
- Drapery Fabricating
- Fabrication
- Fixtures Schedule
- Furnishing Specifications
- General Services Administration (GSA)
- In-House
- Material and Finish Schedule
- Open Office Planning
- Outsourcing
- Package
- Presentation Boards
- Programming
- Project Managing
- Purchasing Agent
- Receiving
- Reconfiguring
- Sales Representative
- Slipcover
- Specialization
- Spending Period
- Subcontracted
- Systems Furnishings
- Tax-Deductible Equipment Package
- Time line
- Total Office
- Universal Design
- U.S. Communities' Master Intergovernmental Cooperative Purchasing Agreement
- Window Design
- Window Treatments
- Workroom

DISCUSSION QUESTIONS

1. Discuss how the size of your community can affect the success of specialization.
2. Consider the many ways in which you can prepare for a specialization in interior design.
3. What areas of specialization do you see coming to the forefront in interior design?

CHAPTER NINE

CERTIFIED SPECIALTY AREAS

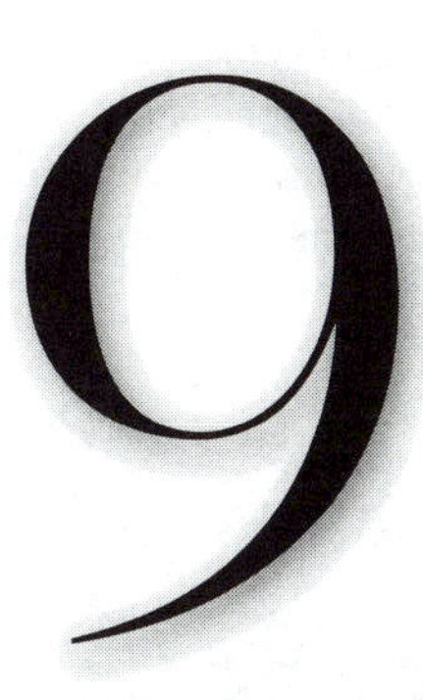

CHAPTER OBJECTIVES After reading this chapter, you should be able to: Understand the importance of becoming certified in a specialized area. Learn more about the specific specialty areas that involve certification. • Understand the procedures necessary for certification.

In Chapter Eight, "Opportunities for Specialization," many areas of specialization were listed and described. However, several of those areas, with further education and experience, can lead to **certification**. There is a distinction between certification and **licensing.** Some states require designers to be licensed before conducting business; in other states, licensing is optional. Certification denotes special expertise, usually through education and/or experience. Many licensed interior designers can also have certification in one or more specialized areas.

Why Become Certified?

Certification gives the interior designer added credibility and status in a particular area of expertise, although not all specific areas of interior design have certification programs.

Our workplace is becoming more regulated, especially in regard to services. Interior design is in large part a service industry; goods trade hands, of course, but designers use skill, knowledge, experience, and creativity to enhance an environment. The real proof of any level of competence is in certification, when applicable. Not all areas of interior design have certification programs and a designer might not have the desire to specialize in a particular area. If a designer's goal is to achieve certification and specialize, the focus of his or her work usually centers on that area because of the amount of experience necessary to complete the program and the continual education required for periodic recertification.

For many designers, carving out a particular niche can be a real career booster. Because of complexities and competition in the marketplace, becoming an expert in a particular area can elevate you in your profession, not to mention on the pay scale. Competition for projects can be extensive so you must set yourself apart. If you are a certified expert in a particular area, you will most likely get the job or project. You can promote yourself and advertise your business as a result of your certification. One of the advantages to becoming licensed or certified is being able to use the **appellation** with your name. Many times it is used in the form of an **acronym,** a series of letters or initials that can be used after your name, indicating you are certified in a particular area.

FIGURE 9.1 Here an interior designer goes over the interior finishes that fit LEED criteria.

SELECTING AN AREA OF EXPERTISE FOR CERTIFICATION

There are many reasons why a designer focuses on a specific area of design. Selecting an area of specialization may be planned as a goal for your career or may come as a result of a particular job. A specialization may cover the job as a whole or add to an extensive project requiring further knowledge. It may also be advantageous for an interior designer interested in filling a void in a particular locale. As a designer, you may have a particular interest or natural ability in a specific area of design. Whatever the reason may be, certification enhances your career.

WHEN TO BEGIN?

There are several stages involved with most certification programs. Education and extensive knowledge come first. Experience through working in the industry is the next component. After this comes the examination phase. Trade associations and professional organizations promote certification and are usually the administrators of the specific programs, each establishing its own criteria for certification. The test is a way to evaluate your knowledge so that the certificate is meaningful and clients can assume that you are an expert in that particular area. The professional organization that establishes the certification process usually provides educational materials, courses, workshops, conferences, mentors, and other resources. They also administer the certifying test. The test for certification can be taken in sections or as one unit. How, when, and where the test is given depends on the size of the organization and the number of people applying for certification. Each state has one or more test-taking sites and each test is given one or more times a year. Within some organizations, pretest workshops are held to help prepare candidates. There is usually a fee for the examination, coursework, workshops, and materials.

CAREER TIP

Certification is primarily for the benefit and gratification of the interior designer.

The application process is also a critical part of certification. Recommendations are usually part of the process and an up-to-date resume listing education and work experience may be required.

In some areas of design, you can begin the certification process as early as college or university study. Leadership in Energy and Environmental Design, for example, conducts workshops for students and others wanting to be certified in LEED. For certification in other areas, you begin with experience running concurrently with education. The **National Kitchen and Bath Association (NKBA)** has affiliations with some universities and coursework monitored by the NKBA is available. There can be several levels of certification as well, each level representing additional years of experience and further testing. The NKBA offers three levels of certification: Associate, Certified, and Certified Master, which are detailed later in this chapter.

Once you receive certification, you must meet continuing education requirements in order to maintain it, renewing annually or biannually. There are associated membership fees and continuing education courses after certification also have fee requirements.

CAREER TIP

Certification instills confidence.

Specific Areas of Certification

Certification gives added credibility to interior designers. A designer can earn one or more types of certification, each indicating a high level of aptitude and knowledge. When a client is looking for particular services, those with certification would be the likely choice. Within these specialty trade associations and certification programs there are added networking opportunities and resources such as: current research, new product information, conferences, and continuing education credits. When project challenges occur, colleagues with certification can be a valuable and extensive support group.

CAREER TIP Certification can make the difference when competing for a job.

FIGURE 9.2 This young professional is studying the necessary material to pass the National Council for Interior Design Qualification (NCIDQ) exam.

KITCHENS AND BATHROOMS

One area of design in which certification is valuable is kitchen and bath. The National Kitchen and Bath Association (www.nkba.org) is a huge trade organization. Within their vast network of members, resources, and practitioners, there is a certification program offering three different levels and you can specialize in both kitchen and bath or each separately. The three levels are:

- **AKBD (Associate Kitchen and Bath Designer).** Requires two years of experience and 30 hours of NKBA coursework or equivalent in an acceptable college program. There is a specific exam for each level and specialty.
- **CKD or CBD (Certified Kitchen Designer or Certified Bath Designer).** Requires seven years of experience and 60 hours of NKBA education or college or university equivalency and an exam.
- **CMKBD (Certified Master Kitchen and Bath Designer).** Requires ten years of experience and 100 hours of NKBA education or college or university equivalency, plus the exam.

To provide the necessary education for passing the exam, NKBA conducts many classes throughout the year. There are also conferences, trade shows, membership and networking, intern programs, competitions, scholarships, and many other resources available to further the specialized career in kitchen and bath design.

FIGURE 9.3 This kitchen was designed by a Certified Master Kitchen and Bath Designer.

FIGURE 9.4 This bath was designed by a Certified Master Kitchen and Bath Designer.

Student affiliation with the NKBA is possible at colleges or universities that have NKBA-approved programs. The student chapter of NKBA enables interested students to get started on their specialization and begin working toward certification in kitchen and bath design while still in school. The benefits to getting started early include networking, focusing work on kitchen and bath design when appropriate, benefiting from mentors and faculty, and meeting the necessary criteria to teach these specialized courses in approved schools. When students graduate from a four-year program, obtaining a bachelor degree, or receive an associate degree from an NKBA-accredited program, they can take the NKBA exam or wait until they have gathered more experience.

There are many successful interior designers who specialize in kitchens and baths and have very rewarding careers. Kitchen and bath design is relevant to most all types of built environments, so the application and need are enormous.

LIGHTING

Another specialization in the field of interior design is lighting. Lighting in our built environments is continually changing due to: new products for energy efficiency; expansion of the types of lighting for different purposes; the highly creative designs of lighting artists; continued research in lighting for health, well-being, and the vision-impaired; new materials and adaptive uses; and many other innovative changes.

Attractive and functional lighting is imperative for all living and working environments. Creative lighting can be an art form. Many exciting and fulfilling careers are focused on lighting, with many and varied applications.

FIGURE 9.5 The carefully planned lighting in Kansas City's Bloch Museum enhances the space while highlighting the artwork.

THE AMERICAN LIGHTING ASSOCIATION

The **American Lighting Association (ALA; www.americanlightingassoc.com)** is another trade association with a certification program that offers several levels of certification determined by exams, training, and coursework; these include:

- **LA (Lighting Associate).** Requires coursework.
- **LS (Lighting Specialist).** Requires coursework and an exam.

- **CS (Certificate Specialist).** Requires expertise that excels and meets requirements in one particular area of lighting.
- **CLMR (Certified Lighting Manufacturers' Representative).** Requires experience and coursework.
- **CLC (Certified Lighting Consultant).** Requires attainment of the highest level of examination and educational credits.

The ALA offers technical courses and educational materials, seminars, testing, and conferences to facilitate its certification programs.

THE NATIONAL COUNCIL ON QUALIFICATIONS FOR THE LIGHTING PROFESSIONS

Another lighting organization with a certification program is the **National Council on Qualifications for the Lighting Professions (NCQLP; www.ncqlp.org)**. This organization not only has testing for a Lighting Certified (LC) designation, but also an intern program for students at approved colleges and universities. Those who complete the lighting internship receive a waiver of some of the experience time necessary to receive certification. Approved lighting interns may use the appellation **"Intern LC."** Their certification process to become an intern involves education, experience, and passing an extensive exam.

Environmentalism

In our efforts to become more responsible about the protection of our environment, many organizations, educational programs, the building industry, and manufacturers all over the world are taking the necessary steps to promote environmental awareness. With this knowledge we are transforming the way we design and the products we use, and changing building principles, practices, and attitudes in general.

FIGURE 9.6 Here is a LEED Gold-accredited commercial showroom.

LEED ACCREDITATION

The **U.S. Green Building Council (USGBC; www.usgbc.org)** is responsible for developing and promoting the **Leadership in Energy and Environmental Design (LEED)** program, a green-building rating system. Under the LEED program, many areas of architecture and design, including new construction, existing buildings, residential and commercial, neighborhood developments, schools, and healthcare, are rated according to measurable building performance.

The LEED program promotes sustainable practices for the benefit of both human and environmental well-being. There are five major areas of concern:

- Energy Efficiency
- Indoor Environmental Quality
- Materials and Resources Selection
- Sustainable Site Development
- Water Saving

LEED utilizes a rating system whereby projects can qualify, be measured, and achieve project certification.

FIGURE 9.7 This LEED-certified residence exhibits resource savings in the areas of energy, water, and waste management.

In order for this program to survive, professionals must have the necessary skills to administer it. Obviously, extensive education, training, and accreditation must be attained to be able to adequately regulate LEED. The **Green Building Certification Institute (GBCI; www.gbci.org)** manages accreditation for building professionals. **"LEED AP" (LEED Accredited Professional)** is the designation for someone who has passed the exam and met all certification requirements. LEED programs include the application process, courses, workshops, reference guides and handbooks, and the exam, provided by the GBCI for accreditation purposes.

Thousands of professionals receive LEED accreditation each year. Many of these professionals are interior designers who choose to design with environmental concerns as their focus and specialty.

Construction Management

Construction management is a professional service involved in the design, planning, and construction of a project. The focus is on quality, time, and money.

Construction management can be a specialization for interior designers. The designer is very knowledgeable when it comes to construction, procedures, scheduling, and the management of projects. There are degree programs in construction management that may be combined with a degree in interior design.

Accreditation for construction managers is through the **American National Standards Institute (ANSI; www.ansi.org).** The actual certification for construction managers is one of the missions of the **Construction Management Association of America (CMAA; www.cmaanet.org).** Thousands of firms and individuals make up the membership of this program.

Certification involves eligibility, the application process, and the exam. As part of the eligibility portion, it is necessary to have four years of experience as someone responsible and in charge of the project. Education and references are also part of the eligibility portion. Going through the application for candidacy and taking the exam comprise the certification process. For more information, go to www.cmaanet.org/cmci.

FIGURE 9.8 LEED-certified buildings for schools help educate young people about future resources.

FIGURE 9.9 This construction manager ensures attention to construction details.

FIGURE 9.10 This very contemporary hospital room suggests a new direction for patient care.

Healthcare

The healthcare industry continues to grow at a phenomenal rate. The design, building, and furnishing of hospitals, clinics, medical offices, and other related facilities have become a huge business. The significance lies not only in the appearance and functionality of these buildings but also in how they can affect the well-being of patients, employees, and guests.

There are many fulfilling job opportunities for designers within the healthcare industry. In addition to basic design skills and knowledge of appropriate materials, functions of specific areas, and space planning, the designer must have a clear understanding of how the medical environment can affect health outcomes.

FIGURE 9.11 Certified healthcare interior designers work on clinic waiting areas to create the most comfortable, relaxing environment for an otherwise stressful situation.

AAHID ACCREDITATION

Certification as an interior designer specializing in the healthcare industry is granted through the **American Academy of Healthcare Interior Designers (AAHID; www.aahid.org).** In order to become board-certified, you must have:

- A college or university degree
- Five years of experience in the healthcare industry
- NCIDQ certification
- Passed the AAHID exam
- A portfolio
- Reference letters

Membership and certification in AAHID is evidence of high achievement and dedication to the field of interior design specializing in healthcare.

FIGURE 9.12 Making the most of technology, this designer illustrates a completed interior before the construction begins.

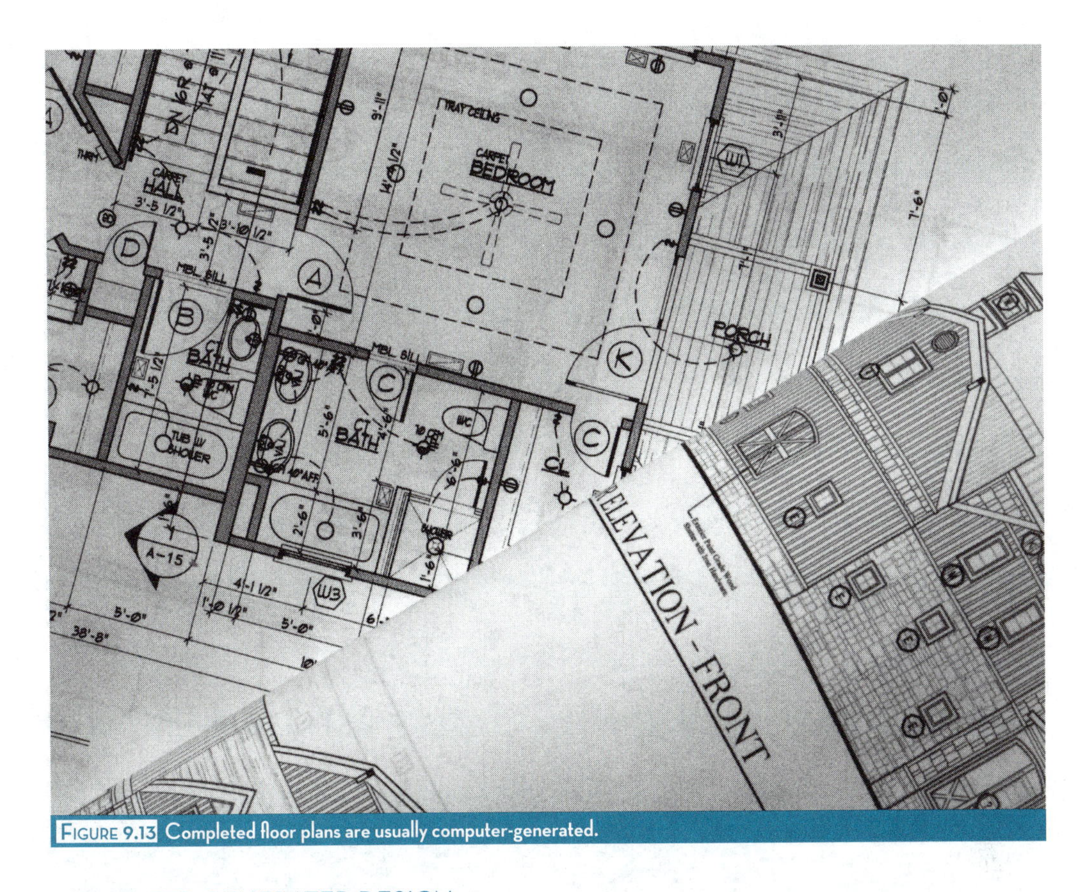

FIGURE 9.13 Completed floor plans are usually computer-generated.

COMPUTER-GENERATED DESIGN

There are an expanding number of software applications in the area of design. There is opportunity for specialization for those designers with skills in applications like Autodesk, Photoshop, AutoCAD, Illustrator, and SketchUp. Autodesk (www.usa.autodesk.com) has a certification program that includes two levels—User and Expert. AutoCAD and AutoCAD Architecture are two areas of certification. The program involves coursework and exams. There are certification centers online and at colleges and universities.

Computer design skills are a critical part of the expertise necessary to become a professional interior designer. Specializing in this can lead to many job opportunities as well as increased income depending on skills and the type of firm you become involved in.

Other Areas of Certification

There are other areas of certification available and many that are being developed at this time.

One specialty area is **feng shui.** The ancient and classical practice of feng shui is used in Asia as well as in

FIGURE 9.14A & 9.14B (opposite page) Feng shui is Chinese for "wind and water," both being major components in this design technique.

many other parts of the world. It encompasses ancient philosophy, elements of nature, placement of objects in the environment, and energy flow—all leading to increased health and well-being. There are many critics of this philosophy as well as many proponents. To be a certified practitioner, workshops, courses, books, and other resources are available. There are several levels of certification as well.

Promoting and adhering to feng shui principles may be a part of an interior design practice or it may be an entire specialty career. There are many books and Web sites detailing the different aspects of feng shui. Clients might ask about it or be very knowledgeable, wanting to apply certain principles but maybe not in the strictest form. Listening and being sensitive to cultural preferences is a very important aspect of interior design. It is the role of the designer to be an advocate for the client, to help them meet their goals, and to preserve and respect cultural differences. It is these differences that help generate great design and enrich the career of the designer.

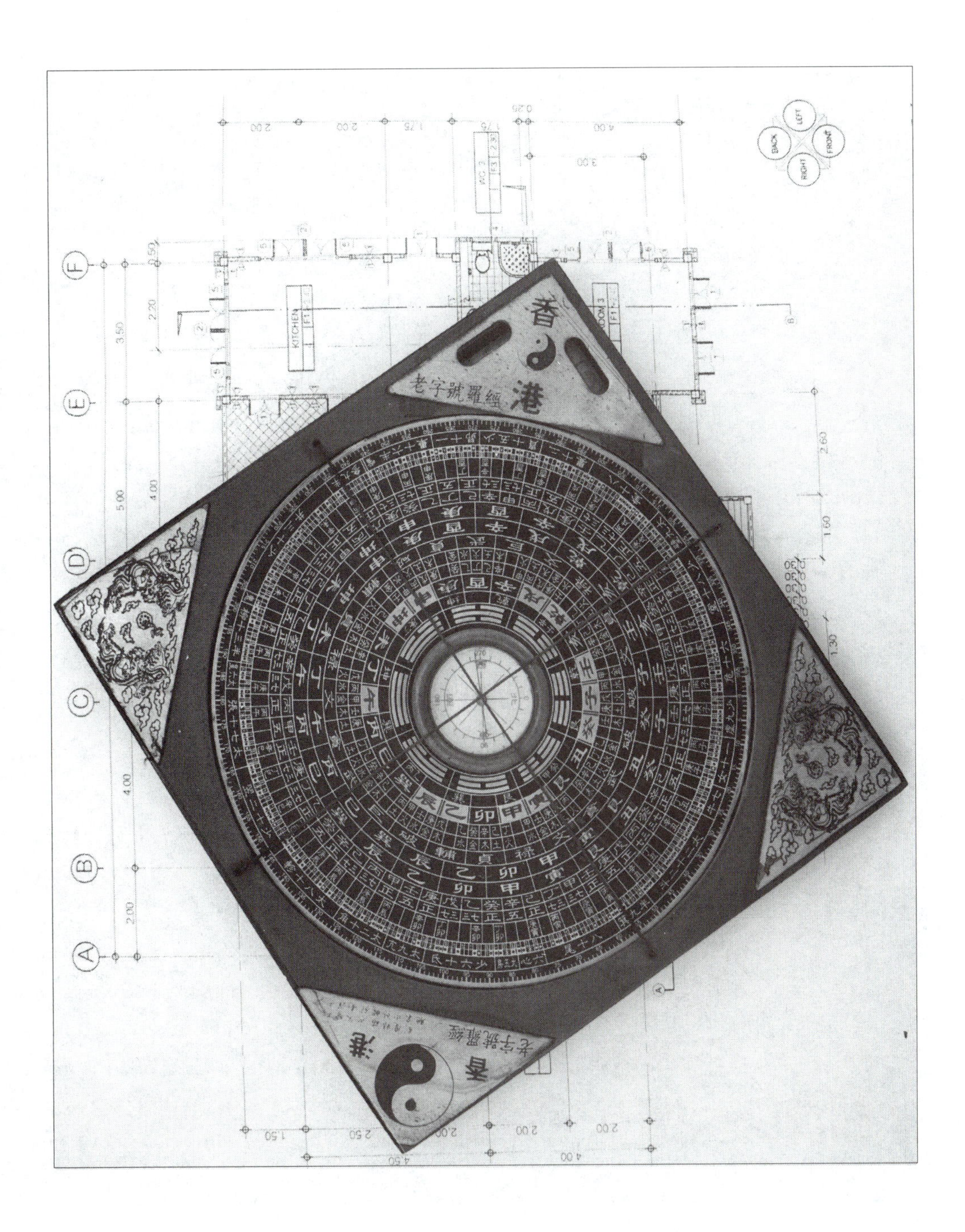
香港
老字號羅經

Interior Designer Profile 9.1: Cheryl Doran, ASID, LEED AP, Interior Designer/Project Manager, Pellham Phillips Architects Engineers, Springfield, Missouri

Cheryl Doran is a senior interior designer with Pellham Phillips in Springfield, Missouri. She has an MA from Webster University in management and leadership and a BS in interior design from Missouri State University. Her affiliations include ASID and LEED; is a board member of the Springfield Design Association, and is a member of the Sunrise Rotary Club. Doran has received many awards, including *417 Magazine*'s Interior Design of the Year, and is a graduate of the Springfield Area Chamber of Commerce's Leadership Springfield program, Class XXII. Doran responded to the following questions regarding specialized certification in Leadership in Energy and Environmental Design (LEED):

Why did you obtain LEED certification?

The impact of designing an environmental building is significant. Commercial buildings annually consume more than 30 percent of the total energy and more than 60 percent of the electricity used in the United States, according to the U.S. Green Building Council (www.usgbc.org). Although LEED certification is not necessary to design a "green" building, it is important to have a standard system that defines and measures "green buildings." I became certified so I could give our clients third-party verification that their building projects meet the highest green building and performance measures.

Have you been able to implement LEED in your projects?

The city of Springfield adopted a "green" policy in 2008 to certify all new construction as LEED Silver. I was the project manager and LEED designer of the city's first project. The new Killian Softball [Stadium] is LEED-certified.

Do you think that special certification is an asset to your work?

More and more the word LEED is becoming a common word in the architectural vocabulary. Clients are becoming more conscious of lowering their operating costs, reducing waste sent to landfills, and conserving energy. They are concerned for employees' health and comfort. Sometimes they qualify for tax rebates, zoning allowances, and other incentives. Being LEED-certified shows our clients that I am committed to helping them be an environmental steward and show a social responsibility.

Did you find the process for certification challenging or educational and how much did it cost?

Visit the Green Building Certification Institute (www.gbci.org) to learn how to become certified and to get a list of the LEED credentialing programs. The process was similar to achieving any certification. I had to register with the U.S. Green Building Council, then register to take my test. The test was given and monitored by a local testing agency, which was very convenient. As soon as you finish your test, you know if you passed or failed. The [LEED] study reference guide for New Construction & Major Renovation v2.2 is 421 pages. A discount is given to students and faculty when purchasing the guide. The education process was challenging because it is a different language. Designing the building "green" is relatively how we have always designed buildings. It [is] implementing the drawings, materials, site, etc. to LEED documentation and the USGBC's system that is time-consuming and challenging. The test to become LEED-certified costs a few hundred dollars with a discount for USGBC members. A new LEED rating system is being implemented and the LEED N.C. v2.2 and LEED CI v2.0 AP exam rating system is being retired. On April 27, 2009, a new version of LEED launched. The ability to be flexible allows LEED to evolve, taking advantage of new technologies and advancements in building-science while prioritizing energy efficiency and CO2 emissions reductions.

SUMMARY

Specializing with certification and licensing enhances your career in many ways and can give you elevated status as a designer. Even if certification is not applicable in your area of specialization, applying the same principles of study to your interests can benefit your career immensely. Professional organizations and educators are developing qualifications and standards in order to create certification programs in many other specialized areas in design. Becoming an expert in your field can result in both monetary and credibility gains.

RELATED CAREER OPTIONS

Related Career Options

- Acoustic Designer
- Art and Accessories Dealer
- CAD Specialist
- Color Consultant
- Communications Designer
- Construction Manager
- Continuing Education Units (CEUs) Administrator
- Corporate Designer
- Designer for Those with Disabilities
- Drafter
- Energy Conservation Consultant
- Environmental Safety Specialist
- Facilities Manager
- Furniture Designer for Healthcare
- Healthcare Designer
- Hospitality Designer
- Kitchen Designer
- Lighting Specialist
- Office Designer
- Product Tester
- Publicist
- Purchasing and Sourcing Agent
- Recreational and Fitness Designer
- Restaurant Designer
- Signage and Wayfinding Designer
- Universal or Transgenerational Designer

SKILLS AND APTITUDES In all areas of certification, commitment to that area of focus is necessary, though the overlapping of areas is natural. Attention to detail, precision, having initiative, and being goal-oriented are some of the many personality traits essential for many of these certified areas. Being decisive and confident, combined with creativity, is important in order to be successful. Keeping up with marketing practices, new products, new materials, and innovative building methods is necessary to keep moving forward in these design areas. Hard work and long hours may be required to finish jobs on a timely basis. Being able to work with many allied professionals is necessary for the project to flow smoothly.

EDUCATION A bachelor degree is always the best way to begin any specialty. Additional education may be required depending on the specialty, but further education and testing are necessary to receive certification. Experience is also a crucial part of the process. Continuing education units (CEUs) are part of the recertification process.

KEY TERMS

- Acronym
- American Academy of Healthcare Interior Design (AAHID)
- American Lighting Association (ALA)
- American National Standards Institute (ANSI)
- Appellation
- Associate Kitchen and Bath Designer (AKBD)
- Certificate Specialist (CS)
- Certification
- Certified Bath Designer (CBD)
- Certified Kitchen Designer (CKD)
- Certified Lighting Consultant (CLC)
- Certified Lighting Manufacturers' Representative (CLMR)
- Certified Master Kitchen and Bath Designer (CMKBD)
- Construction Management Association of America (CMAA)
- Feng Shui
- Green Building Certification Institute (GBCI)
- Intern LC (Intern, Lighting Certification)
- Leadership in Energy and Environmental Design (LEED)
- LEED Accredited Professional (LEED AP)
- Licensing
- Lighting Associate (LA)
- Lighting Specialist (LS)
- National Council on Qualifications for the Lighting Professions (NCQLP)
- National Kitchen and Bath Association (NKBA)
- U.S. Green Building Council (USGBC)

DISCUSSION QUESTIONS

1. Analyze the job opportunities in your area of the country and discuss how certification could enhance your ability to find employment and increase your wages.
2. What are some steps that you could take in order to decide whether or not specialization is right for you?
3. Discuss the benefits of attending conferences and going to trade shows relative to your interest in a specialized area of design.

CHAPTER TEN
PROFESSIONAL DEVELOPMENT

10

CHAPTER OBJECTIVES

After reading this chapter, you should understand how to enhance your professional position in order to secure and maintain the job through methods such as: Strengthening Your Unique Qualities • Entrepreneurialism • Portfolio Development • Résumé Refinement The Interview Keys to Success.

Professional development is not a career ladder that you can ever completely scale; there is always one more step. It continues indefinitely as the industry advances, global connections expand, cultural definitions become blurred, and societal customs change.

It is up to you to get ready for that continual climb; build your stamina, practice persistence, always look forward, and do not remain static or settle for the status quo. We are constant learners and the momentum increases regardless of how much education and experience we have had. Your degree in interior design is the first step. Academics prepare you for the **experiential** education, but before you take those shaky initial steps, make sure that you have your persona perfected.

Your first job as an interior designer is to work on yourself and your image. Design is about visuals; your client or employer sees you first, then your presentation. They may give you the job based on the image that you portray rather than on stacks of past work.

Every career in interior design has a sales component. Selling yourself is first and foremost. You sell yourself: your character, your personality, and then your talents and abilities. Clients need or want your **expertise** in creating and enhancing their environment. Your expertise could be in any of the following areas: conceptual, product knowledge, applications, job management, planning, or a combination of these and other things, including knowledge, experience, and capability. Sell yourself first and your expertise will sell itself. Look in the mirror and at your work and absolutely love what you see. If you don't, make changes until you see what you want others to see.

FIGURE 10.1 This very confident interior designer projects a strong professional image.

CAREER TIP Invest in a classic suit and make sure that the fit is perfectly tailored. It is easy to change "the look" with simple accessories.

Strengthen Your Unique Qualities

Be unique in your interior design career. Professional designers who have striking qualities are more marketable and consequently make more money than those who have fewer notable or outstanding qualities. A potential employer or client should see something, such as your presentations and/or designs, that shows great potential and makes you stand out. That exceptional and very individual quality may just be a client's reason for deciding to hire or work with you. If you cannot pinpoint a specific quality, develop one, and then another, and another.

BE YOURSELF

As you develop your individual personal style, it never hurts to experiment a little. Try different approaches, stretch a little, read biographical material of successful designers, and imagine how the employer will see you.

BE EXCEPTIONAL

Exceptional knowledge or specialization in a particular area could be your strongest resource. A unique quality can be anything that sets you apart from the rest. Additional knowledge about a specific field or specializing in an area of interest is always helpful. There could be a quality about the way in which you work or approach your projects that is unique. Being thought of and remembered in a positive way is helpful in career-building. A consistently positive attitude and a warm personality are two traits that are hopefully not that unique but are definitely sought after. Many times, it is your personality that is the basis for the employer's final decision. A friendly, pleasant, smiling personality can win over employers and clients alike.

FIGURE 10.2 This designer appears extremely pleasant to both clients and peers.

DIVERSIFY

For a new college graduate, one way to be unique is to have more than one major or area of study. Some areas that complement interior design are: construction management, landscape architecture, art, business, communications, advertising, marketing, global studies, and psychology. Bringing an additional skill or skills to a job could make the difference when competing with even more experienced interior designers. For every new skill or ability that you acquire, many more opportunities will follow.

BE ORIGINAL

It is a normal progression for interior designers to acquire additional knowledge as they work on various jobs. When an interior designer does a high-end residential project successfully, the neighbors will know about it and more jobs of the same type will follow. One important element to consider is how to be continually creative and original for each individual project. Two jobs that look the same in any area will create problems for future success. Designers need to constantly look for aspects on every project that are unique to only that project. Interior designers should take every opportunity to design something unique for their clients. Dare to be different.

FIGURE 10.3 This custom design makes this job unique from any other.

The same is true in the commercial industry. For example, designers who successfully work with healthcare soon get labeled as healthcare designers. The more work that you do in a specific area, the more you learn, and the more of an expert you become. When an area of interest becomes your expertise, it is extremely important to become completely knowledgeable in that area. You are the trusted expert.

STAY CURRENT

One of the most important aspects of a career in interior design is to know what is currently on the market, where to find it, and how to get creative and adaptive with that information. Interior design, like most careers, requires constant continuing education, both in and out of the classroom. Read, research, and travel to major markets. Keeping up with the changes in new materials, technology, and the industry is extremely important. Changes in the industry are also what keep the profession interesting and exhilarating. Continually look around, not for anything particular; just observe and keep your eyes open for new and interesting ideas and inspirations. There are always new things to discover and fresh ideas to implement—new products for old uses and new uses for old products.

FIGURE 10.4 Current periodicals offer inspiring articles and ideas.

It is fun to take note of new ideas and businesses that are related to interior design. There are many innovative, clever, and fun businesses. The real estate company HomeVestors of America, Inc., known for their "We Buy Ugly Houses" billboards, sells homes with great potential, for example. Or what about creating a business that upholsters furniture in new ways, making the sofas and chairs look like art and/or fashion forms? What about a furniture company where all the floor samples and in-stock items are covered in muslin, waiting on a custom cover selection for quick delivery, or an interior design company that specializes only in holiday designs? These appear to be great income-producing ideas and are all very unique and individual. Use your skills and imagination to come up with a specialty business of your own. What fun!

FIGURE 10.5 A good first impression is very inviting.

SPREAD THE WORD AND THE IDEAS

The communication of ideas, verbal and otherwise, is a very beneficial and marketable skill. If you, as a person with lots and lots of ideas, can quickly sketch an idea and communicate it to your client, then decisions can be made and your project will proceed more rapidly. Time is money, and efficient communication skills and presentation techniques advance your reputation and career. Even if it is a simple, spontaneous sketch, your client will feel more secure because of the visual communication. Both designer and client will agree that the design solutions are mutually understood if they can be seen beforehand. If you are a designer charging by the hour, not only will your clients like how much money you saved them and know and understand what you are trying to convey but they will be happy to relate your efficiency to other potential clients. An enhanced client list leads to enhanced income.

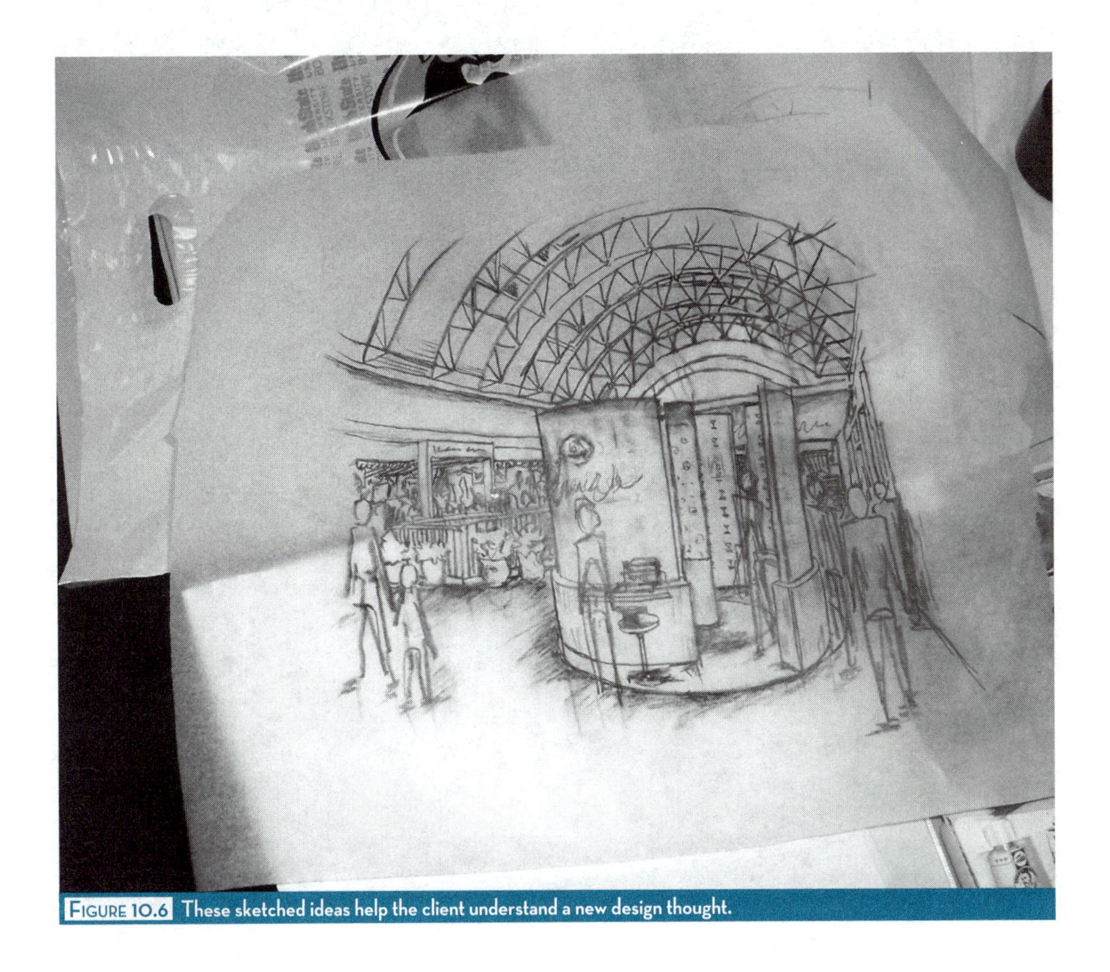

FIGURE 10.6 These sketched ideas help the client understand a new design thought.

VIRTUAL REALITY

For a growing number of interior designers, technology has broadened their ability to communicate. Computer-aided design (CAD) offers an enormous range of presentation tools, such as: floor plans, elevations, perspective drawings, and even animations of completed buildings while in the planning stages. These can also show the specified color and materials. Clients love virtually walking through their proposed new building and seeing what the potential results could be. What a dynamic sales tool! There are many software programs that can enhance visual communication.

FIGURE 10.7 A realistic computer-aided graphic can be a great selling tool for a new project.

IF YOU SEE BEAUTY IN THE TIRED AND WORN . . .

Designing new uses for old materials, including buildings and/or building parts, is another way to highlight your unique talents and design ideas. Sometimes it is something from the past that gives us inspiration to create something new or to give new life to something that already has a history. It might be a sad and lonely old building, a pile of discarded remnants from a house long abandoned, or even Grandmother's rocking chair that gives you renewed purpose. Finding new uses for old materials and abandoned spaces is not the same as historic preservation, which is a separate and specific specialization. **Historic preservation** can provide a client tax incentive, signal the beginning of gentrification for a developer, trigger the revitalization of an entire community, and/or offer the interior designer a specialty with great rewards and sometimes difficult challenges to be met and conquered.

Interior design for existing buildings creates many different types of jobs and is a great source of revenue for the design industry. Interior design is often thought of as the icing on the cake. When a new home or commercial building is complete, many times the budget has become so stressed that the nonstructural items, such as interior design, are put off until a later time and, unfortunately, never get completed. For this reason, working on older, existing buildings, both residential and commercial, can be more profitable for the interior design professional.

THERE ARE NO LIMITS TO UNIQUENESS

There are so many ways that you can choose to be unique in your career. Taking an opportunity to design almost anything for the interior is one of the easiest. It could be a tile configuration for a wall or floor, a custom area-rug design, or a custom design in any resilient or carpeted floor. It might be a special ceiling design, a different use for a material, an unexpected item displayed like an art piece, or even a designed "dress" for

FIGURE 10.8A & 10.8B The before and after of this historic renovation show the amount of work necessary for an interior design of this nature.

a chair. The advantages to being an original interior designer seem pretty obvious. However, you would be amazed at how often designers fail to utilize innovative thinking. Creative people need to find interesting ways to solve design problems. Many times a problem or challenge demands the greatest amount of creativity and ultimately becomes the greatest achievement. In our very global and competitive world, having a creative mind sets you apart and gives you a definite advantage. To be successful these days, you need to be special. Find it, develop it, and use it.

GET NOTICED AND MAKE A POSITIVE IMPRESSION

Getting a job and keeping the job require uniqueness and individuality. Consider the type of business, corporation, or CEO who is making the decision, and direct your attention there. There is no substitute for getting the approval of whoever is really in charge. If the president or **CEO** of a company says they do not make the decisions, it is usually because they do not want to hire you. In reality, the person at the top can influence any decision within the company, although he or she is also extremely busy and hard to get an audience with. Nevertheless, the higher you go up the chain of command for your interview, the better your chances of being hired. Remember that old adage: "It is not what you know, but who you know."

If you are having trouble getting that first interview, don't be afraid to be special and unique from the very beginning.

FIGURE 10.9 Designers spend time with potential clients.

After several attempts to get an appointment with the president of a company, a talented designer stopped by to visit with his secretary about bringing lunch in for a brief meeting. While in the office, the designer took mental notes about the colors and decor. The secretary arranged a lunch time in the president's office, with the understanding that the president could stay only a short time. The designer had a catering company prepare a hot but simple lunch, including salad and dessert, which would fit in an easy-to-carry basket along with china, glassware, cloth place mats, and napkins that matched his office. A florist created a small, fresh flower arrangement for the centerpiece. All of this was easily and fashionably carried in by one person—the interior designer.

The fresh flowers and an outline of the intended business were left with the potential client after the lunch meeting ended. Needless to say, the company president was very impressed! He even asked his secretary to come in and take pictures of the pretty luncheon display. The designer no longer had to worry about the company knowing how her interior design business could be helpful with new projects.

Using your special talents becomes a way of life and a natural part of who you are, and the wonderful designer that you will become.

Professionalism

One more time, remind yourself: "You never get a second chance to make a good first impression." How you present yourself can be very positive for business, it can be just so-so, or it can be damaging. If you want to be respected as a businessperson, you must act and look like one, and it is never too early to begin refining yourself.

ATTIRE

Many companies have what is called "casual Friday." What if you are meeting with a new client for the first time on Friday? Casual is not acceptable unless you would make the client uncomfortable by dressing up.

There are interior designers who work with their clients wearing blue jeans. Are they as casual about their work as they are about their attire? There are designers who are commonly seen in high-end "designer" jeans with very upscale tops and accessories. This might work depending on the clientele. Be aware that the "designer" look does not need to be expensive, only creative or artistic, neat, and stylish. Name-brand clothing is not necessary, but quality is important. Remember, if you obviously care about how you present yourself, your client will feel that you care about your work as well.

Know the key elements of dressing for success. Suits are great and do not need to be pin-striped. A variety of clothing ensembles can portray success, professionalism, and of course "designer." Do not wear too much jewelry or other distracting elements. Keep in mind that you are not dressing for dates or recreation. Classic designs are always safe and do not have to be too conservative.

Dressing for interior design presentations is another consideration. Complement the presentation. It is not necessary to match your presentation, but enhance it. If your presentation is primarily green, be careful not to introduce an additional color of green in your clothing. Make your presentation look good, and look good with your presentation.

Interior design professionals spend time at dirty job sites, workrooms, and sample rooms with lots of thread and lint, paint, and finishing products. Keeping this in mind, it is a good idea to keep extra shoes in your

FIGURE 10.10 These designers are dressed in very appropriate attire for their individual profiles.

automobile or bag and even a change of clothing or a cover-up item handy. Do not get too comfortable and forget to change back to the professional look. It is better to overdress than to underdress.

A dark or bold suit in black, navy, or red is great for a committee meeting or board meeting where you are presenting yourself and the interior design contract for approval. Keeping the eyes on you and your presentation is your goal in this situation. If your audience is looking at you, they might be listening to you as well, but at least they will believe that you know what looks good. Black or red colors work well for dark hair and eyes. Your best suit color might be navy blue if you are a blond with blue eyes. The suit needs to be dramatic on you. Having a color profile done can be very helpful, even for a person knowledgeable about color.

FIGURE 10.11 This interior designer dresses for success regardless of the type of job.

NEAT AND CLEAN

Having a positive, original, and professional manner will help create and show your uniqueness in this very artistic career. As an interior designer, create a package that includes your look and your personal style, which includes your **portfolio** presentation style.

Designers always pay attention to detail and sometimes it is the little things that are noticed. Keep your bag, purse, or briefcase in good condition. Shoes should be appropriate and polished. Even your car should be clean and well-maintained. Every aspect of your appearance can make an impression.

PERSONAL ATTRIBUTES

Consistency is a plus. When someone wants to know what you are like as a designer, what will people say? Will they say it depends on what day it is or if you have gotten prepared? We should do our best to be our best every day. Put a smile on your face and you might receive one back. We cannot always help how we feel; however, we can help how we act. Most of us enjoy working with pleasant people. A negative personality is never acceptable—not with your coworkers, clients, reps, or the public in general.

Designers communicate visually with their boards and samples, but they also do so verbally. Making eye contact, speaking distinctly, using proper grammar, diction, avoiding slang, and speaking to be heard are all aspects of professional verbal communication.

Body language can reveal a lot. Facial expressions, the way you fold your arms, and the way you sit in a chair or stand can make an impression. Your manners while dining, introducing others, and shaking hands; telephone etiquette; and conversational etiquette can make or break a job interview and help or hinder your client relationship. Learn to relax and try to stay calm during these interactions. Take a deep breath, be confident, and fold your hands in your lap (try not to talk with your hands except to make an occasional point). Written communication is equally important. Proper language, word usage, punctuation, and sentence structure should reflect an educated person. Timeliness in response to e-mails, telephone calls, and letters, in addition to punctuality, is critical. Thank-you notes are always appreciated.

Preparation for a career in interior design requires more than study. All of your personal attributes combined with your education and experience help create the professional designer. It is never too early to begin to develop yourself in order to fulfill your highest potential.

CAREER TIP Always have a notebook, camera, and tape measure by your side, in your bag, or in your car. You might want to add thumbnail sketch paper (also referred to as "trash paper") to this list. Clients enjoy seeing you draw on the job with trash paper.

Entrepreneur

Interior design careers offer a great many ways and opportunities to be an **entrepreneur.** This is primarily true because there are so many different kinds of interior designer (e.g., interior designer, interior decorator, registered interior designer, licensed interior designer, interior architect).

Within each of these areas, there are many subcategories and different levels and ways to develop a successful career.

Initially, working for an interior designer or related business would allow you to see a variety of areas that you could develop into your own future business. Even as an employee in an interior design firm or related business, you are likely to establish your own clientele. Clients that are assigned to you by your employer will become your clients. If you leave that place of employment, the client that you have been working with will more than likely follow you, providing that you are doing a great job and have established a good working relationship. In many interior design firms, it is each designer's responsibility to acquire his or her own clients. People work with people. For this reason, many interior design firms require a **noncompete clause** in their employment contract. This usually states that when an interior designer or product salesperson leaves a company, they cannot work in a specified area for a specified number of years. The point here is to know what is in your contract.

While working for an interior design firm, one can also find the area or areas that are most personally satisfying and/or profitable. You might begin formulating ideas about beginning a business emphasizing or specializing in that product or area of expertise. Some examples of these are: custom drapery or window treatments, computer-aided designs, kitchens and baths, linens, fireplace designs, or even outdoor spaces. The list goes on and on.

FIGURE 10.12 This company's specialty is fabric for custom drapery and upholstery.

Interior design, like many other industries, can also be a home-based career. It is not necessary to have a showroom for furniture and accessories to be successful in this business. Having an office separate from your residence is best for separating your business from your private life, but this two-in-one option does offer minimal **overhead.** When an interior designer works with businesspeople doing commercial interiors, it usually works best to have a convenient workplace for meetings both with clients and sales representatives. This could still be your residence if it were thoughtfully planned.

There are many critical decisions to be made during design projects. The desire for beautiful and functional environments and the benefits of having design help have resulted in the public's choice to hire interior design professionals. Designers are problem solvers and the right solution is critical to the success of the project: the right color choice for a classroom to enhance learning, space planning to encourage family interaction, and selecting sustainable materials instead of materials that have a negative impact on the environment are examples of making the right choice. The added awareness of custom interior spaces, introduced through advertising and several television programs, has also brought interior decorating and design to the attention of more people. Many previously thought hiring an interior designer was reserved only for the rich and elite. Television reality shows are another entrepreneurial venture that has become an interior design career.

FIGURE 10.13 This home office, bathed in natural light, is ideal.

There are strong interconnections across the spectrum of design industries (e.g., home furnishings, fashion, automobiles, paper products, linens). Many product designers adopt some elements of current trends and styles to use on their respective products. Color trends being the same in housing and fashion, and similarity in patterns, regardless if they are in apparel or upholstery, all reflect these connections. Developing full-spectrum design, relating to all of basic consumer products, is another entrepreneurial avenue to pursue. The connections between all these industries are becoming greater all the time, with each industry influencing the other and changing at a very rapid pace. The consumer can hardly keep up with the new trends, products, colors, and styles. How about becoming a **trend forecaster**?

FIGURE 10.14 These products coordinate with each other and with up-to-date patterns.

FIGURE 10.15 This window treatment was inspired by a fashionable evening gown.

Specific abilities are necessary if you are to be an entrepreneur or own your own business. Here are a few to begin cultivating (and a business minor would be helpful):

- Decisiveness
- Leadership qualities
- Managerial skills
- Organizational skills
- Self-motivation and persistence

There are an infinite number of ways to use your design education and experience and they can be applied to almost any facet of life and profession. There are no boundaries.

Portfolio Development

The portfolio is a sales tool and a portrait of you as a professional. Your portfolio will get you the job, a job, or an audience. Building a portfolio is a necessary and valuable asset in acquiring employment with a design firm. It sells your abilities and design capabilities to a client and captures the attention of a potential client, who will remember your work for future consideration.

Interior designers are creative, imaginative, and artistic. The portfolio of an interior designer should be at least that and more. Determine what it is about your presentation that will impress someone and make you stand taller than the rest, and then emphasize those aspects. Interior decorators, interior designers, and licensed or registered interior designers all have creative abilities that set them apart; express them, show them, and definitely flaunt them.

CAREER TIP Make your own portfolios or journals of specific examples that you like. Tear pages from your own magazines, sketch an idea, take a picture, and add favorite colors—all are great ways to create notebooks. This can be a tool you can turn to when you get "stuck." It's fun to create journals specific to areas such as painted items and rooms, outdoor spaces, small spaces, window treatments, kitchens and bathrooms, or simple design details.

A PORTFOLIO IS A FORM OF COMMUNICATION

Drawings, presentation boards, illustrations, and sketches are all forms of visual communication—a translation of words into a pictorial format. A portfolio is a compilation of these visuals, a representation of past or intended work. It enables the designer to present the skills, creativity, and talents that he or she possesses to a client or employer. Words cannot always convey what a picture can: inspiration, emotion, energy, uniqueness, style, and so on. A successful portfolio can impress on many levels; sometimes "seeing is believing."

THE PORTFOLIO AS DESIGN SOLUTION

Interior design is about creating successful design solutions. Think about a portfolio as a design solution. Portfolios are a sales tool, a presentation of work and abilities, and an excellent opportunity to highlight your special talents. After all, you are the creative design person, so design your portfolio. As you consider your portfolio's potential, be mindful that:

- Adapt and tailor your portfolio to fit particular job applications, adding and deleting to focus on a particular job type.
- It is never too early to begin thinking, planning, compiling, and assembling your portfolio.
- Make it count. The presentation of your portfolio may be the only opportunity to make a visual statement in the pursuit of the perfect job.
- Remember, the portfolio is a portrait of you—make it beautiful.
- You are never finished developing your portfolio. Keep adding, changing, and improving it as your career progresses. It evolves as does your career.
- Your portfolio is not something that you throw together just before graduation or just before the first interview.
- Your portfolio should reflect your own particular style.

"A picture is worth a thousand words" is a saying that we have heard all our lives and it is especially true in the business of interior design. Interior design is all about visuals and how what we see in our environment

FIGURE 10.16 An interior designer practices a presentation in front of the office staff.

affects us. As you develop your portfolio, think about how this visual presentation will affect the viewer. Is the work exciting, refreshing, and inspiring? Is it sophisticated, full of creative ideas and talent? Try to look at your work as someone would for the first time. Have your designer contacts and peers examine and critique your portfolio before you present it for a job interview or to a potential client. Practice your presentation and gain confidence.

THE PORTFOLIO AS DOCUMENTATION OF PRIOR WORK

Whether you are a student or an interior design professional, your portfolio should show your interior design job presentations as well as your completed works. Photographing the completed job provides **documentation** and proof of actual job experience. It is easy to forget some of your work experience, but pictures can help map your professional career. When an interior design job is finished, photographing the completed job also provides the client with an opportunity to say "thank you" one more time and provides confirmation that the client is satisfied with the outcome. It is a perfect way to complete the job and leave the door open for future work with that client.

FIGURE 10.17 This unique presentation attracts the client's attention.

MULTITALENT MULTITASKING

Variety, comprehensibility, and flexibility in what you as a designer can offer are important to represent in your portfolio. Interior designers have a long list of services that they can provide. Showing examples of as many of these as possible will enhance your portfolio and job opportunities. An employer or client cannot possibly know the broad range of your talents, so it is up to you to convey that information to them, in the most visual way possible.

A very short list of the services an interior designer can provide a client might include:

- Assemble the needed allied professionals. Be the mediator between the client and the project team. Be a diplomat.
- Create sample boards, drawings, and floor plans. Be an illustrator and artist.
- Develop the design concepts for the project. This requires knowledge infused with creativity.

FIGURE 10.18 Photographing the completed project while visiting with your satisfied client is a great way to complete a project and ensure positive feedback.

FIGURE 10.19 Sharing a variety of presentation styles with potential clients creates a lasting impression.

- Ensure quality workmanship. Be an inspector.
- Interpret the client's needs and establish a list of goals. This requires good listening skills.
- Keep abreast of new and innovative products, materials, finishes, and applications. Be a researcher.
- Manage the implementation of the design project. This requires organizational and management skills.
- Prepare a budget, schedules, and specifications. Research current pricing and availability. Be an accountant.

IMAGINATION IS NOT JUST FOR THE YOUNG

When you consider portfolio ideas, think about different formats. There is no one right way to create your "brag board." Begin by trying to come up with some clever way to attract attention and display your work. An imaginative example is a lampshade with a presentation on it if you specialize in lighting, or a letter-sized box or specially designed bag that could have information about you and your abilities all over the inside and outside. How about a custom-designed calendar that could incorporate portfolio information and also provide business-card information for easy reference? For a global connection, try a hand- or hanging scroll with pockets for project illustrations and pictures. Consider a piece of specially designed art that could impart portfolio information as well. The format should be as creative as you are, so take the opportunity, even if it is a slight risk. Questionable is better than mundane. You want to be noticed and remembered.

TECHNOLOGY STREAMLINES PORTFOLIO DELIVERY

Digital presentations should be extremely well-done. They should be just as good as any other kind of presentation; once again, creativity is the key. Technology can provide that "wow" factor if done with skill and imagination. If your technological skills are less than great, seek professional presentation assistance. Digital presentations are easy to mail or e-mail; however, keep in mind that a face-to-face encounter is a key element in providing an effective presentation and is important in the final decision-making process. Also, when doing a digital presentation, bring your own laptop to prevent awkward delays or inconveniences. Practice your presentation in front of others and plan to relax.

It is extremely difficult to keep presentation boards in great shape; however, having some actual interior design presentation board available, in addition to the digital information, could be beneficial. Something tangible and up-close can add another layer of interest. If an employer has read about you, held your presentation boards, looked at you and your work on a CD, and has had the opportunity to sit down and talk with you, eye to eye, chances are you won't be forgotten.

KEEP SIMPLE AND STREAMLINED

Simplicity is another approach. Potential employers or clients are very busy and do not want to wade through excessive pages, descriptions, and papers. A very nice portfolio binder or folder can be eye-catching and show photographs extremely well. There are many creative ways to bind presentation pages into a book format. Always make color copies and offer to provide as many presentations as required to get the job. As you move through the hiring process, several meetings may be necessary. Be eager and willing to interview at each hiring level. It should not be necessary to leave a portfolio behind. Your résumé and cover letter are perfect items to have for the file. Portfolios are very much a part of you and your creative ideas, and are not meant for an employer's permanent record unless you have a digital component that is easy to leave. One drawback to the very portable digital portfolios is that they are easy to pass around or copy—and not always with permission. Make sure that you leave your work in reliable hands.

Presentation boards can look pretty tacky after setting them around your office or taking them to several client meetings. They should not be left with your client until the job is complete. You can have presentation boards framed and matted. Frames can look very attractive and can protect your work. You can then easily maintain that crisp edge and fresh look. Frames could have your **logo** permanently attached, and a replaceable label area for your client's name.

As the interior design professional, you hold the keys to your portfolio. Present yourself as you want to be viewed by your audience. Keep in mind the old cliché "you never get a second chance to make a good first impression."

FIGURE 10.20 This presentation model shows very precise detail.

Résumé

Keep your résumé simple. A one-page, creative, and easy-to-read résumé will get attention. Interior design professionals are often stereotyped and assumed to look a certain way. So if you look the part and think it would be to your advantage, add a picture of yourself. Do not use lengthy explanations to describe yourself or your experiences. Make sure your information is current, to the point, and relevant. Keep your résumé positive. You are talented and skilled and that is the story that needs to be told. Make yourself look good by avoiding clichés and worn-out buzzwords. This is not the time to be humble; instead, show off and highlight your best and most definitive skills.

Many current books on the subject can help you write an effective résumé. Also, the Internet and tools like the computer application Microsoft Office Publisher have good articles and templates to help with formatting.

The résumé, like your portfolio, is a reflection and definition of you—your education, experience, objectives, and goals. Keep your résumé updated and adjust it for different job applications. Know a lot about the company or firm with which you are applying and tailor your résumé accordingly. An exceptional résumé can open doors for you or slam them shut. Be diligent, exact, eye-catching, and creative. It is your first step; don't make it the last.

SUCCESS BREEDS SUCCESS

The more successful you appear, the more success you will have. When you succeed, ask your client, employer, or professor to give you a written note for the purpose of sharing or selling yourself. This documentation could be a note, quote, or letter of reference. These notes or letters can be used to enhance a portfolio. Keeping a list of awards, a "thank you" or compliment file, a list of professional organizations with which you are affiliated, or any other type of professional accomplishment inventory is a good idea for anyone furthering his or her career. Keep in mind that visuals are still the most important. Most firms or potential clients are not going to want to spend lots of time reading about you. They want to see your qualities, and it doesn't hurt to show how others have responded to your work. The résumé might be a place to mention a few of these past successes.

The Interview

The interview can take place in a variety of ways: person-to-person, on the phone, via a **conference call**, online, with a meal at a restaurant, or at any other place and in any other way convenient for the employer. Informing yourself about the company, client, or employer is essential. We have already addressed attire and personal demeanor, but keep in mind that how you present yourself visually can make an indelible impression—make it a positive one.

PHONE INTERVIEWING

The phone interview has its own set of concerns. Here are a few important points to remember when interviewing on the telephone:

- Anticipate the questions that will be asked and make notes of your answers.
- Be a good listener so you can thoroughly answer the questions that are asked.

- Don't be afraid of a moment's silence and don't be tempted to ramble on to avoid those short breaks in the dialogue.
- Have a scheduled time for the interview, so you are not caught off guard.
- Let the employer take the lead and control the interview.
- List on a piece of paper the important and relevant facts that you want the employer to know about you.
- Make arrangements to answer the call where you are most relaxed and not distracted, and where there is not a lot of background noise.

There are many good references on the subject of interviewing over the phone, in person, and via the Internet. Regardless of how or where the interview is conducted, preparation, forethought, and composure determine the effectiveness and the eventual outcome.

FIGURE 10.21 These project team members obviously enjoy working together.

Keys to Success

When I was on my high-school yearbook staff many years ago, we used to chant: "Simplicity is the key to success." Simplicity applies to most careers. "Less is more," a quote by architect Ludwig Mies van der Rohe, is another overused quote, but one that says so much, regardless of the context. Try to do what you do well, then expand or branch out. One of the biggest mistakes designers make is to take on too much. Keep the workload manageable and reasonable. It is better to do one job well than two jobs only halfway.

One of my college professors always said: "Depend on experts in their field." There are so many experts who are necessary to complete an environment for living or working. Knowing what the end result needs to be like does not make us an expert in every area. Basic knowledge makes some people dangerous. We all need to let the electricians, plumbers, engineers, and other professionals do their jobs and work with them as though everyone is on the same team. Team members are most successful when they complement each other's abilities. Remember, "No man is an island." Many times, it is the designer who is responsible for co-ordinating this group of specialists and acting as a mediator between the client and the other professionals. Be an advocate for your clients and they will reward you.

A HAPPY CLIENT IS A FUTURE CLIENT

Do not pass up an opportunity to put that last finishing touch on a job and make sure that your client is satisfied. As the designer, your goal should be to hear that loud applause, receive that pat on the back, and accept that well-deserved "thank you." Your client's response should be an important part of completion and is necessary for job satisfaction. Money is not always the primary motivator for hard work. Success is a great motivator and reward in itself. We need to make sure our clients are satisfied and impressed with our interior design delivery.

VISUAL JOURNAL FOR THE CLIENT

One very professional way to leave an excellent reminder of a job well-done is to create a notebook or visual journal of the job and present it to the client. It is a great resource for future information: notes, before-and-after pictures, sources, names and numbers of materials and finishes, specifications, dimensions, even ideas for future improvements. Your client will appreciate the fact that the quality of the finished project was important to you as well. Often the client will refer to those pages, plans, or sketches when further changes are being made. The client will often "show off" the journal to impress others with the improvements and efforts put forth.

BROADEN YOUR REPERTOIRE

Many times, the designer is a problem solver: when the material is discontinued, when unexpected problems arise, when the price for a product doubles, and on and on. The designer must turn these challenges into opportunities for creativity. Often, your best work comes as a result of having to think independently, with originality and problem solving and critical thinking skills.

Keep your eyes and ears open to learn all you can about the cultural differences in our society and others. The world is a much smaller place than it used to be and many communities have a growing and diverse population. As a designer, you need to meet the different cultural needs of these varied people and respect

FIGURE 10.22 Cultural differences can present fabulous learning experiences.

their heritage, beliefs, and lifestyles. We need to do our part in preserving our clients' rich cultural heritage, artifacts, designs, and ways of life. And the client isn't the only one to benefit here; as you improve their living and working environment, they can enrich your life.

Success is usually measured by how much money you make, but that is only one component of success. The most important measure of success is how happy you are with your career. If your client or employer is satisfied with your job, you will gain their confidence and respect. Fortunately, with interior design, there are many, many ways to apply your skills and knowledge. If one area of design does not satisfy you, try another. According to research, the average college student changes his or her major 3.8 times and the average worker changes jobs many times as well. The field of interior design is wide-open and the opportunities are growing by the minute. Designers are gaining respect and moving into related fields. Specialty areas continue to grow as a result of technology, globalization, and the mainstreaming of **green design** and **sustainability.** It is interesting to watch it all unfold and it is a good time in our history to be an interior designer. It is a very rewarding career in a multifaceted way. When you share that enthusiasm with those around you, it can only enhance your extraordinary career.

SUMMARY

Preparing for success in interior design encompasses all areas of your persona. Your natural attributes, education, and experience blend seamlessly in order for you to become a highly talented and respected professional. The scope of the profession is broad and the rewards are great. It all depends on you; invest in yourself, get to know your clients, be flexible, and work hard.

RELATED CAREER OPTIONS

Acoustic Designer
Adaptive Reuse Specialist
Art Sourcing Agent
Color Consultant
Corporate Designer
Drafter
Furniture Designer
Government Designer
Graphic Designer
Historic Preservationist
Hospitality Designer
Illustrator
Journalist
Landscaping Designer
Manufacturer's Representative
Marketing And Merchandising Professional
Office Designer
Product Designer
Publicist
Real Estate Broker
Renderer
Residential Designer
Restaurant Designer
Restorator
Retail Designer
Teacher
Textile Designer
Window Treatment Designer

SKILLS AND APTITUDES Communicating with your employer or client is essential. You have to be a good listener and sometimes play the role of psychologist in order to determine what it is that the client wants. You have to be a mediator—between client and contractor, allied professionals, coworkers, employer and staff, and even married partners. The goal is to meet the wants and needs of everyone involved. Do your best in difficult situations.

Being creative can really elevate you in this business. It is sometimes the particular set of problems that inspires the creativity. So be a problem solver.

There are hundred of decisions to be made on design projects. The overwhelming number of choices is what propels most people to hire a designer in the first place. The designer often narrows down the field of choices so the client can then make a personal choice.

Attention to detail is one of the skills that a good designer develops. It is sometimes the subtleties that make the difference in the overall outcome of the project—the details that tie the different elements together, create the harmony between parts, and complete the whole.

Being able to work with all types of individuals and situations necessitates an open and friendly personality. Be genuinely interested in your clients, be considerate, respect their budgets, and honor their wishes.

Be ready to continue to learn. This field is ever-changing, from new products and materials to popular styles and trends, research, technology, consumer demand, and better-informed consumers. All contribute to the need to stay current.

The skills necessary to be a successful designer include learning to draft, drawing to scale, measuring and calculating, being able to visualize the intended plan, and developing the ability to create all sorts of visuals. The computer aids designers as well, with all sorts of software and the vast resources to be found on the World Wide Web.

There are many more ways to prepare for a design career, especially regarding education. Experience can sometimes be the best teacher. You can start with part-time jobs, job shadowing, summer work, or internships; any type of related work will help. You can never be too prepared, so get started and be the best that you can be, for yourself and your clients.

Interior Designer Profile 10.1
Christine A. Lehman, Interior Design Student, Missouri State University

Christine A. Lehman is a perfect example of how to get on the fast track to success. Lehman is taking all the necessary steps in order to ensure a successful career in interior design. In addition, she brings to this effort many talents and personal attributes such as determination, organizational skills, an exceptional work ethic, and beauty inside and out.

Lehman is a highly motivated college student. She is actively pursuing a bachelor degree in interior design. Her list of accomplishments is lengthy. She has maintained a position on the dean's list throughout college, received many scholarships, and won several design competitions. She is the current ASID student chapter president and is a member of the College of Natural and Applied Sciences Student Advisory

Board at MSU. She is a member of the Phi Eta Sigma Honor Society, Rho Lambda Honor Society, and Alpha Delta Pi Sorority.

Lehman attends workshops, seminars, and NeoCon (a trade show featuring product and service exhibitors for the design of corporate, hospitality, healthcare, retail, residential, and other design projects). She has been on an MSU-sponsored trip to China and has gone to Italy and Greece as well.

To lend insight into her success, Lehman shares the following list of her thoughts and opinions:

- Choose to seek a degree in interior design because of a love of a related personal interest—in my case, drafting and space planning. After working with an interior designer, my career choice was obvious.
- Identify goals. My goals for an interior design career include creating and restoring environments, inspiring clients, and "spending each day getting to do what I love."
- Study hard and go out into the real world; get your hands on real work experience and network. Networking gets you the work and experience improves your ability as a designer. Experience with clients builds your confidence and communication skills.
- Try your hand at some of the actual physical work on projects. I found this a beneficial experience, although I acknowledge this approach may not appeal to everyone.

EDUCATION A four-year degree from an accredited college or university is the first step. Further education in specialized areas will help, depending on your career goals. Preparing for the NCIDQ exam, taking continuing-education classes, and self-learning all contribute to your knowledge base.

KEY TERMS

Chief Executive Officer (CEO)	Documentation	Green Design	Overhead
Conference Call	Entrepreneur	Historic Preservation	Portfolio
Digital Presentation	Experiential	Logo	Sustainability
	Expertise	Noncompete Clause	Trend Forecaster

DISCUSSION QUESTIONS

1. What are some steps you can take to expose yourself to all sorts of design?
2. Discuss some rules of professional etiquette: dining, office, communication, and attire.
3. Discuss ways to professionalize your portfolio and résumé, and prepare for the interview.

GLOSSARY

A

ACRONYM. A word formed from the first letters of several words, such as ADA, which stands for Americans with Disabilities Act.

ADAPTIVE REUSE. When a building or property is changed or redesigned to be used for another purpose.

AESTHETICS. The philosophy, study, or theory of beauty.

ALLIED PROFESSIONALS. Professionals who participate in the design and construction of a building.

AMBIENT LIGHTING. Diffuse and uniform lighting for general illumination.

AMERICAN ACADEMY OF HEALTHCARE INTERIOR DESIGNERS (AAHID). An organization offering certification in healthcare interior design.

AMERICANS WITH DISABILITIES ACT (ADA). An official act of the U.S. government composed of federal, state, and local regulations that prohibit the discrimination against people with disabilities.

AMERICAN LIGHTING ASSOCIATION (ALA). An organization for lighting professionals.

AMERICAN NATIONAL STANDARDS INSTITUTE (ANSI). An organization that oversees the development of voluntary standards for products, services, and processes in the United States.

AMERICAN SOCIETY OF INTERIOR DESIGNERS (ASID). The leading national organization for interior designers in the United States.

ANTHROPOMETRICS. The study and comparison of human body measurements.

APPELLATION. A name or title, or special designation.

ARCHITECT. The engineer of structures and buildings.

ART BROKER. One who buys and sells art for clients and dealers.

ART GUILD. Trade association based on apprenticeship and control standards to protect the members and the craft.

ASSOCIATE KITCHEN AND BATH DESIGNER (AKBD). A level of certification for kitchen and bath designers.

ASSOCIATION OF REGISTERED INTERIOR DESIGNERS OF ONTARIO (ARIDO). A self-regulatory professional organization for interior designers in Ontario, Canada.

B

BARRIER-FREE DESIGN. A design in which there are no physical obstacles for someone with a disability and/or using a wheelchair.

BIDDING. Providing the price of a product or service.

BIG-BOX STORE. Large retail store offering competitive prices.

BOUTIQUE. A small specialty shop.

BREACH OF CONTRACT. The instance of breaking a contract by noncompliance.

BUILDING CODE. A federal, state, or local regulation that applies to a building's health and safety.

BUILT ENVIRONMENT. The environment that is built by man (buildings for whatever purpose).

C

CALL CENTER. The customer service communication hub of a business, as in a credit card company's call center.

CERTIFICATE SPECIALIST (CS). A level of lighting competency gained through experience and testing, usually in one particular area of lighting.

CERTIFICATION. Proof of a level of proficiency, usually by experience and/or examination.

CERTIFIED BATH DESIGNER (CBD). A level of certification for bath designers.

CERTIFIED KITCHEN DESIGNER (CKD). A level of certification for kitchen designers.

CERTIFIED LIGHTING CONSULTANT (CLC). A level of certification for lighting designers.

CERTIFIED LIGHTING MANUFACTURERS' REPRESENTATIVE (CLMR). One who is certified in lighting design and represents lighting products for one or more companies.

CERTIFIED MASTER KITCHEN AND BATH DESIGNER (CMKBD). A level of certification in kitchen and bath design.

CHANGE ORDER. A document that states a change in the placement of an order for goods or services.

CHIEF EXECUTIVE OFFICER (CEO). The highest-ranking officer of a large company, responsible for carrying out the policies of the company.

CLIENT. The person(s) or company for whom you provide services.

COALITION. A union.

CODE. Federal, state, or local regulation established for the health and safety of the public.

COLOR PSYCHOLOGY. The study of how color affects one's emotions.

COLORIST. One who selects colors for products.

COMMERCE. Trade in goods and services.

COMMISSION. A fee paid to an agent.

COMPUTER-AIDED DESIGN (CAD). A design that is generated with the use of a computer.

CONFERENCE CALL. A telephone call made concurrently to more than one person.

CONSTRUCTION MANAGEMENT ASSOCIATION OF AMERICA (CMAA). An organization representing the construction management profession.

CONSUMERISM. A pre-occupation with and an inclination toward the buying of consumer goods.

CONTINUING EDUCATION UNIT (CEU). The academic unit attached to educational courses or workshops.

COST-PLUS. Pertaining to billing, the cost of a product or construction plus a percentage.

COUNCIL FOR INTERIOR DESIGN ACCREDITATION (CIDA). The accrediting body for interior design higher education in the United States and Canada.

CUBICLE. A partitioned work area in a room.

CUSTOM. Designed specifically for the project.

D

DEMOGRAPHIC. Relating to population statistics.

DESIGN. The planned arrangement of basic principles and elements to create an environment, product, or work of art.

DESIGN CONCEPT. A general idea or solution for a project: how it will look, function, and be used.

DESIGN ELEMENTS. The basic components of design: line, pattern, texture, light, scale, and color.

DESIGN PRINCIPLES. The basic principles of design: scale, rhythm, emphasis, proportion, balance, and harmony.

DESIGN PSYCHOLOGY. The study of design and its effects.

DIGITAL PRESENTATION. A presentation created with the use of a computer.

DOCUMENTATION. The process of providing written details or information about something.

DOWN PAYMENT. A certain percentage of the price of goods or services paid at the onset of a project or before special orders are made.

DRAPERY FABRICATION. The making or construction of drapery.

DYE LOT. A single run of color printing or dyeing using a particular batch of dye. Dye lots may vary in color.

E

ENTREPRENEUR. One who initiates or finances new commercial enterprises.

ENVIRONMENTAL DESIGN. Design in consideration of the natural world or a person's surroundings.

ENVIRONMENTAL PSYCHOLOGY. The study of the effects of a person's surroundings.

ERGONOMICS. The study of the human form and movement in relation to furniture and other products.

ERRORS AND OMISSIONS INSURANCE. Insurance to cover mistakes in a contract.

EXPERIENTIAL. Relating to, providing, or based on experience.

EXPERTISE. The skill, knowledge, or opinion of an expert.

F

FABRICATION. The making of a product.

FAMILY EDUCATIONAL RIGHTS AND PRIVACY ACT (FERPA). A federal law that protects the privacy of student education records.

FEDERAL TRADE COMMISSION. A United States federal governmental agency created in order to prevent unfair business practices.

FENG SHUI. An ancient Chinese philosophy with implications for design.

FIRE RESISTANCE. The ability of a material to resist flammability.

FIXED-FEE RATE. An established rate or amount of payment for services.

FIXTURES SCHEDULE. The time frame or scheduling for the installation of fixtures in a building.

FRANCHISE. The license to sell a company's products.

FURNISHING SPECIFICATIONS. A detailed list of the furnishings for a project: the source, information, and description.

G

GENERAL SERVICES ADMINISTRATION (GSA). An organization that, in addition to other functions, develops cost-minimizing policies for government buildings and their furnishings.

GENTRIFICATION. The transformation of an aging neighborhood or part of town into a prosperous one through remodeling and reinvestment.

GLOBALIZATION. The act, process, or state of operating on a global scale.

GRANDFATHERED. To be exempt from a new legal ruling.

GREEN BUILDING CERTIFICATION INSTITUTE (GBCI). An organization that sets standards for construction that embodies environmentalism.

GREEN DESIGN. Design that is concerned with protecting the quality of the environment.

HEADWALL. The main wall of focus, or the wall one faces.

HISTORIC PRESERVATION. The process of returning a building to its original condition while maintaining its style, materials, and intent.

HOURLY FEE. Payment for services rendered based on a dollar amount per hour.

HVAC SYSTEMS. The heating, ventilation, and air-conditioning system in a building.

I

IMPLEMENTATION. The act of carrying out or fulfilling.

IMPLIED WARRANTY OF FITNESS. An implied warranty for the suitability of something for a particular purpose.

INDEPENDENT SUPPLIER. A provider of merchandise or products who is not subject to control by others.

IN-HOUSE. Used to describe a service or product provided within the company.

IN-HOUSE DESIGNER. A designer employed by a company to design its own properties.

INDEPENDENT PRACTICE. The business of a person who is self-employed.

INDOOR AIR QUALITY. The condition of the air in a building.

INDUSTRIAL DESIGN. Design in industry, production or manufacturing.

INTERIOR ARCHITECTURE. A term to indicate the planning and design of interiors.

INTERIOR DESIGN EDUCATORS COUNCIL (IDEC). An organization of interior design educators.

INTERIOR DESIGN EXPERIENCE PROGRAM (IDEP). A program that provides methods of assessment and documentation to quantify one's work experience in preparation for the NCIDQ exam.

INTERIOR DESIGNERS OF CANADA (IDC). An official organization of Canadian interior designers.

INTERN DESIGNER. A student or apprentice designer who is acquiring experience in order to prepare for a career in interior design.

INTERN LC. A lighting intern—a student or apprentice who is gaining experience in order to achieve certification.

INTERNATIONAL FEDERATION OF INTERIOR DESIGNERS/ARCHITECTS (IFI). Provides a forum for international discussion among design professionals, currently in 45 countries on every continent.

INTERNATIONAL INTERIOR DESIGN ASSOCIATION (IIDA). An organization of interior designers from all over the world.

INTERNATIONAL RESIDENTIAL CODES (IRC). One of many sets of codes established for residential construction that provides for the safety and welfare of residents.

INTERNSHIP. The placement of a student or apprentice in a work situation in order to get experience in interior design.

J

JOINT AND SEVERAL LIABILITY. Shared responsibility for damage.

JUNIOR DESIGNER. A mid-level designer in a firm.

L

LAMINATION. A process of bonding layers of thin material to form a composite material.

LEADERSHIP IN ENERGY AND ENVIRONMENTAL DESIGN (LEED). A rating system for buildings in regard to green design.

LEED ACCREDITED PROFESSIONAL (LEED AP). A person who has become certified in LEED design through examination.

LETTER OF AGREEMENT. A written document or contract that states which services are to be rendered in a design project, the parties involved, the time frame, payment, rights, and termination of the contract.

LIABILITY WITHOUT FAULT FOR DESIGN DEFECTS. An obligation under law for costs and/or damages.

LICENSE. A permit or legal authorization to perform services or own something.

LICENSED INTERIOR DESIGNER. A designer who has a permit to practice interior design in a particular state or region.

LIFE-CYCLE COSTING. Calculating the total cost of an item by dividing its purchase and maintenance price by the expected years of use.

LIGHTING ASSOCIATE (LA). A level of certification in lighting design.

LIGHTING SPECIALIST (LS). A level of certification applied to lighting professionals.

LOBBYIST. Someone who lobbies political representatives on an issue.

LOGO. A design symbolizing an organization, used for advertising and name recognition.

LUMINAIRES. Lighting fixtures.

M

MATERIALS BINDER. A notebook or binder used to outline and organize a project.

MATERIAL AND FINISH SCHEDULE. A detailed list and description of all the materials and finishes to be used on a project.

MATERIAL STANDARDS. The basic model or quality for acceptable material to be used in a design project.

MERCHANDISERS. Those who engage in commerce or trade of goods or commodities, buying or selling.

MILLWORK. Wood trim, stock and custom, used for shelving, cabinetry, and molding.

MISREPRESENTATION. To give a false idea or portrayal of something.

N

NATIONAL COUNCIL FOR INTERIOR DESIGN QUALIFICATION (NCIDQ). An interior design certification earned after formal education and experience. Passing the NCIDQ exam is also part of this process.

NATIONAL COUNCIL ON QUALIFICATIONS FOR THE LIGHTING PROFESSIONS (NCQLP). A council to monitor the qualifications of certified lighting designers.

NATIONAL KITCHEN AND BATH ASSOCIATION (NKBA). A trade organization specializing in the design of kitchens and baths.

NONCOMPETE CLAUSE. An agreement not to compete in business for an established amount of time.

O

ONE OF A KIND. Only one model or object is created.

OPEN OFFICE PLANNING. A concept of interior design that eliminates walls.

OUTSOURCING. The process or act of transferring work to an outside company to reduce costs.

OVERHEAD. The expenses necessary to conduct business.

P

PACKAGE. A number of different components combined to constitute a unit.

PERFORMANCE TESTING. Refers to subjecting a material or product to testing in order to determine how that product performs.

PORTFOLIO. The representation of creative work via sample projects, drawings, or photographs.

PRESENTATION BOARD. A form of visual communication using drawings, such as floor plans, elevations, samples of materials, and other information, to help a client visualize a project.

PRIVATE SPACES. Spaces in a building or home in which privacy is warranted, specifically bedrooms and bathrooms.

PRODUCT LIABILITY. The producer's legal responsibility for damage or injury caused by goods.

PRODUCT SALE. The sale of something made or created.

PROFESSIONAL NEGLIGENCE. Carelessness and irresponsibility in a profession.

PROFIT MARGIN. The amount of money earned after all expenses have been paid.

PROGRAMMING. The gathering and analysis of information for an intended design project.

PROJECT MANAGER. One who organizes and ensures completion of a project.

PROTOTYPE. An original sample product used to assess, fit, design, construct, and produce.

PROXEMICS. The study of the spatial needs of people, which vary depending on culture and personal preferences.

PUBLIC SPACES. Those areas designed for the public or guests to congregate.

PUNCH LIST. A final list of all the remaining items to be completed on a project.

PURCHASING AGENT. A person whose job it is to do the buying for a company.

R

RECEIVE. To take a product delivery.

RECONFIGURE. To rearrange or change parts for a particular use.

REGISTERED INTERIOR DESIGNER. An interior designer who is registered with the state in which he or she does business. Different criteria are used to establish registration requirements per state.

RENDERERS. The artists who draw the proposed building, usually in perspective and often in color.

RENEWABLE. Materials that can be reproduced in a sustainable and timely manner.

RENOVATION. The act of restoring, or making like new.

RESILIENT FLOOR MATERIALS. Flooring materials that have some give or bounce when compressed.

RETAINER FEE. A fee used to reserve professional services.

RETRO. Modeled on something from the past.

RETROFIT. To modify something with new parts.

S

SALES AGENCY. A franchise to sell something.

SALES REPRESENTATIVE. A person who represents a company or product line with the intent of selling those products.

SATISFACTORY. Good enough to meet a requirement.

SCHEDULE. A chart that describes the materials used on building surfaces (inside and out) and includes windows and doors.

SEASONAL AFFECTIVE DISORDER (SAD). A condition associated with an individual's inadequate exposure to sunlight.

SENIOR DESIGNER. A designer in a firm who has either by talent and/or length of employment risen in status within the company.

SITE ORIENTATION. The position of a building in relation to such natural elements as sun and wind.

SLIPCOVER. A detachable cover for an upholstered piece of furniture.

SOLAR ENERGY. Energy from sunlight that can be used for heat or electricity.

SOLE PRACTITIONER. A person who, alone, operates his or her business.

SOLE PROPRIETORSHIP. The state of being the sole owner of one's business.

SOURCING. Production capacity outside the source of origin.

SPECIALIZATION. Expertise.

SPECIFICATIONS. The written list of furnishings and materials to be used on a project, itemized, described, and sourced.

SPENDING PERIOD. An allocation of time to use a corresponding allocation of funds.

SQUARE FOOT. A two-dimensional measurement using length and width. Length multiplied by width equals square foot.

STANDARD. An established level of quality.

STATE CODES. Rules or regulations specific to each state.

STATE LICENSE. The license or permit to work in a particular state.

STRIKE. To cease to work as a protest.

SUBCONTRACT. A secondary contract in which the person or company initially hired hires someone else to do the work.

SUSTAINABILITY. The ability of a design to limit its impact on the environment, thereby sustaining that environment for future generations.

SYSTEMS FURNISHINGS. A flexible type of component furniture that can be arranged to accommodate various needs.

T

TASK LIGHTING. A type of lighting that targets a specific object or task .

TAX-DEDUCTIBLE EQUIPMENT. Equipment used in business or manufacturing in order to conduct business; the cost can be deducted from profits for taxation purposes.

TEXTILES. A general term used to refer to fibers, yarns, or fabrics.

THE DESIGN ASSOCIATION (UK). This society, with members in 34 countries, holds a British Royal Charter for accrediting and representing professionals in many fields of design.

TIME LINE. A chronological chart of events or tasks in the execution of a design project.

TOTAL OFFICE. Used to describe office systems that can provide all components for a complete office.

TREND FORECASTER. One whose responsibility it is to look to the future and predict consumer choices.

TRUNK SHOW. A limited showing of new products by a company representative.

U

UNION. An organization of workers.

UNIVERSAL DESIGN. An interior design concept that requires spaces and furnishings to meet the needs of individuals regardless of age and ability.

U.S. COMMUNITIES' MASTER INTERGOVERNMENTAL COOPERATIVE PURCHASING AGREEMENT. A buying agreement for nonprofit organizations, thereby reducing costs.

U.S. CONSUMER PRODUCT SAFETY COMMISSION (USCPSC). A governmental agency charged with ensuring the safety of products in the marketplace.

U.S. GREEN BUILDING COUNCIL (USGBC). A national organization that promotes sustainability and green design in construction.

VISUALIZATION. The ability to form a mental image.

VOLATILE ORGANIC COMPOUNDS (VOC). A compound found in many products, such as solvents and adhesives, that produce toxic fumes and gases that are released into the air, but dissipate with time.

WALK-THROUGH. A thorough check after the completion of a job to make sure all contracted work is complete.

WAYFINDING. The use of signage or other colors or materials to assist a person in finding his or her way in a building.

WHITE NOISE. Background noise.

WINDOW DESIGN. The design of store windows and their displays in order to attract customers.

WINDOW TREATMENTS. Materials placed on windows for aesthetics, privacy, insulation, or the blockage of sunlight.

WORKROOM. A facility for the fabrication of window treatments, upholstery, and other products for a design project.

CREDITS

FRONT MATTER
page vi Tim Klein/Getty
page viii Rob Melnychuk/Getty

CHAPTER 1
page 1 © Pete Leonard/Corbis
page 2 Stockbyte/Getty
1.1 © Ruth B. Tofle
1.3 Dennis MacDonald/World of Stock
1.4 © Pete Leonard/Corbis
1.5 © Jack Lacey/Corbis
1.6 © Jupiterimages
Profile 1.1 Photo courtesy of Marian Chase

CHAPTER 2
page 23 Rob Melnychuk/Getty
page 24 Robert Daly/Getty
2.1 Juice Images
2.3 Maxim Petrichuk | Dreamstime.com
2.4 © Andy Dean/Fotolia.com
2.6 © Karen Melvin/Corbis
2.7 Patti McConville/Getty
2.8 Unlisted Images, Inc. © 2010
2.9 © Fotolia XXIII/Fotolia.com
2.10 Red Cover/Alun Callender
2.11 Digital Vision Photography/Veer
2.12 Rob Melnychuk/Getty
2.13 © Daniel Hopkinson/Arcaid
2.14 Red Cover/Guglielmo Galvin
2.15 Red Cover/Amanda Turner
2.16 Photographer Santos-Diez/fabpics/ Arcaid. Architect: CDG Arquitectos.
2.17 Bernhard Lang/Getty
page 50 Gary Buss/Getty

CHAPTER 3
page 53 Johh Gollings/Arcaid.co.uk
page 54 Cobbett/Getty
3.1 © imagebroker/Alamy
3.2 Photograph Courtesy of Kohler Co.
3.3 Tess Stone/Getty
3.4 PhotoAlto/Alix Minde/Getty
3.5 Morley von Sternberg/Arcaid.co.uk
3.6 © Corbis
3.7 Saylor H. Durston; COPYRIGHT © 2010 THE CONDÉ NAST PUBLICATIONS
3.8 John Gollings/Arcaid.co.uk
3.9 Ableimages/Getty
3.11 © Emily Hagopian/Arcaid
3.12 Kei Uesugi/Getty
3.14 Comet Photography/Veer
3.15 SIMON KENNY/CONTENT
3.16 Photo © Brett Boardman
3.17 Copyright Bass Pro Shops
page 78 Todd Warnock/Getty

CHAPTER 4
page 83 © Charles Davis Smith/ Architect, RTKL Associates Inc.
page 84 Seth Joel/Getty
4.1 © Larry Lefever Photography/ Architect, RTKL Associates Inc.
4.2 © Archimage/Alamy
4.3 Design & Photos by Joe Kesterson-Claude Neon Federal Signs Tulsa, OK
4.4a PAUL TYAGI/VIEW Pictures
4.4b Design: Sheppard Robson. Photographers: Hufton + Crow.
4.5 AAGAMIA/Getty
4.6 © Charles Davis Smith/Architect, RTKL Associates Inc.
4.7 © 2009 Barry J. Grossman Photography/Architect, RTKL Associates Inc.
4.8 © Jeffrey Totaro/Architect, RTKL Associates Inc.
4.10 © Sabrih|Dreamstime.com
4.11 altrendo images/Getty
4.12 © Jeffrey Totaro/Architect, RTKL Associates Inc.
4.13 © Crodenberg | Dreamstime.com
4.14 © Auris | Dreamstime.com
4.16 Kym Browning, info@canzdesign.com, CanzDesign.com. Date: 10/30/2008; subject: Bonita Del Rey Dental Office.
4.17 Seth Joel/Getty
4.18 Andersen Ross/Getty
4.19 © John Connell/Corbis
4.21 © Michael Jenner/Corbis
page 107 altrendo images/Getty

CHAPTER 5
page 111 Digital Vision Photography/Veer
page 112 Stuart O'Sullivan/Getty
5.1 © 2010 JupiterImages
5.2 © Art Directors & TRIP/Alamy
5.3 Loungepark/Getty
5.4 Tooga/Getty
5.5 © Stéfan Le Dû
5.6 Getty Images
5.7 Getty Images
5.8 Solus Photography/Veer
5.10 Digital Vision Photography/Veer
5.11 Courtesy of Harem & Company
5.12 David Oliver/Getty
page 128 Bruce Ayres/Getty

CHAPTER 6
page 131 Jill Rohrbach/Arkasas Department of Parks and Tourism
page 132 Tim Robberts/Getty
6.1 Steve Curtis of Space Design Studios www.bardesign.co.uk
6.2 Image and the Crowne Plaza® Hotels and Resorts name appear Courtesy of InterContinental Hotels Group.
6.3 © Hotel Prinsenhof
6.4a Kerry Kraus/Arkasas Department of Parks and Tourism
6.4b Jill Rohrbach/Arkasas Department of Parks and Tourism
6.5a © Alise O'Brien
6.5b © Alise O'Brien
6.6a Photography by Michael Kleinberg for Loews Hotels
6.6b Photography by Michael Kleinberg for Loews Hotels
6.7a Hotel del Coronado.
6.7b Hotel del Coronado.

6.8 © View Pictures Ltd/SuperStock
6.10 Madonnina Del Pescatore Restaurant. Photo © Michele Tabozzi.
6.11 UpperCut Images/Getty
6.12 Thomas Northcut/Getty
6.13 Photograph by: Jennifer Dana Deane
page 153 Emportes Jm/Getty

CHAPTER 7

page 157 © auris/Fotolia.com
page 158 Matthew Ward/Getty
7.1 Yasuo Murota/Getty
7.2 Kate Brady/Getty
7.3 Keren Su/Getty
7.4 B & M Productions/Getty
7.6 Ed Reeve/Getty
7.7 © Cultura Limited/SuperStock
7.8 TONY LINCK/Getty
7.9 Red Cover/Huntley Hedworth
7.11 © auris/Fotolia.com
7.14 MoMo Productions/Getty
7.15 © Avital Aronowitz
7.16 Red Cover/Jean Maurice
Profile 7.1 Photo courtesy of Jeff M. Walker
page 180 Joe Cornish/Getty

CHAPTER 8

page 185 © 2008 Lukas A Bryson (Boise,ID) www.lab7media.com
page 186 Tay Jnr/Getty
8.1 Comstock/Getty
8.2 Courtesy Elizabeth Turner's curtain workroom in West Sussex
8.3 UNLISTED IMAGES, INC © 2010
8.4 Photo courtesy of Haworth Inc.
8.5 Courtesy of Herman Miller, Inc.
8.6 Courtesy Steelcase Inc.
8.8 Fernand Ivaldi/Getty
8.10 © 2008 Lukas A Bryson, (Boise, ID) www.lab7media.com
page 204 UpperCut Images/Getty

CHAPTER 9

page 209 Michael Moran; COPYRIGHT © 2010 THE CONDÉ NAST PUBLICATIONS
page 210 © Sundikova|Dreamstime.com
9.1 Jim Arbogast/Getty
9.2 Image Source/Getty
9.4 Andersen Ross/Getty
9.5 PHOTOGRAPHY: ANDY RYAN. DESIGN: STEVEN HOLL ARCHITECTS.
9.6 Photography by J. Miles Wolf © 2009. Interior Design: Jodi Bruemmer of Kurt Platte Architects. Architecture: Mark Gunther of Wichman/Gunther Architects
9.7 Photography by J. Miles Wolf © 2009. Architecture and Interior Design: SHP Leading Design.
9.8 Photography by J. Miles Wolf © 2009 Robert Ehmet Hayes & Associates, PLLC in addition to CMTA Engineers.
9.9 Jon Feingersh Photography Inc/Getty
9.10 © Jeffrey Totaro/Architect, RTKL Associates Inc.
9.11 Provided by FKP Architects, Photography Hester + Hardaway
9.12 Picturenet/Getty
9.14 Michael Moran; COPYRIGHT © 2010 THE CONDÉ NAST PUBLICATIONS
page 231 Roger T. Schmidt/Getty

CHAPTER 10

page 235 Jupiterimages/Getty
page 236 Mash/Digital Vision/Getty Images
10.1 Digital Vision Photography/Veer
10.2 Jon Feingersh/Getty
10.3 Steffen Oeser, Elise Boyer and Rob Metke
10.4 © Avital Aronowitz
10.5 Michael Melford/Getty
10.6 Photo by Holly Murdock, sketch by Karamie Maynes.
10.7 AAGAMIA/Getty
10.8a Design by Lauren Liess, Pure Style LLC, www.thepurestyle.com
10.8b Design by Lauren Liess, Pure Style LLC, www.thepurestyle.com
10.9 Yukmin/Getty
10.10 Jupiterimages/Getty
10.11 Somos/Veer/Getty
10.12 Image100 Photography/Veer
10.13 © Roger Brooks/Beateworks/Corbis
10.14 Red Cover/Henry Wilson; designer: Maria Speake
10.15 DreamPictures/Getty
10.16 © UpperCut Images/SuperStock
10.17 © Avital Aronowitz
10.18 © UpperCut Images/SuperStock
10.19 © UpperCut Images/SuperStock
10.20 hana/Datacraft/Getty
10.21 Eric Audras/Getty
10.22 Red Cover/Paul Massey
page 266 Jon Feingersh/Getty

COLOR INSERT

color plate 1 © Daniel Hopkinson/Arcaid
color plate 2 Red Cover/Guglielmo Galvin
color plate 3 Red Cover/Amanda Turner
color plate 4 Saylor H. Durston; COPYRIGHT © 2010 THE CONDÉ NAST PUBLICATIONS
color plate 5 John Gollings/Arcaid
color plate 6 Ableimages/Getty
color plate 8 (left) PAUL TYAGI/VIEW Pictures; (right) Design: Sheppard Robson. Photographers: Hufton + Crow.
color plate 9 © Art Directors & TRIP/Alamy
color plate 10 Tooga/Getty
color plate 11 GettyImages
color plate 12 Madonnina Del Pescatore Restaurant. Photo © Michele Tabozzi.
color plate 13 © 2008 Lukas A Bryson, (Boise, ID) www.lab7media.com

INDEX

Page numbers in italics refer to figures.